D0753543

# TROPICAL GRASSLANDS

Ben Morgan

**www.heinemannraintree.com**
Visit our website to find out more information about Heinemann-Raintree books.

**To order:**
☎ Phone 888-454-2279
📠 Visit www.heinemannraintree.com to browse our catalog and order online.

Published in 2011 by Heinemann-Raintree books, an imprint of Capstone Global Library, LLC, Chicago, Illinois

© 2011 The Brown Reference Group Ltd.

For The Brown Reference Group Ltd:
Editorial Director: Lindsey Lowe
Managing Editor: Tim Harris
Editor: Jolyon Goddard
Original consultant: Dr. Mark Hostetler,
Department of Wildlife Ecology and Conservation, University of Florida
Designers: Reg Cox, Joan Curtis
Picture researcher: Clare Newman
Production Director: Alastair Gourlay

Printed in the USA

ISBN: 978-1-432-94182-6; 978-1-432-94184-0 (set)
14 13 12 11 10
10 9 8 7 6 5 4 3 2 1

**Library of Congress Cataloging-in-Publication Data**

Morgan, Ben, 1968-
  Tropical grasslands / Ben Morgan.
    p. cm.—(Biomes atlases)
  Includes bibliographical references and index.
  ISBN 978-1-4329-4182-6 (hc)
  1. Grassland ecology—Tropics—Juvenile literature. 2. Grassland ecology—Tropics—Maps for children.  I. Title.
  QH541.5.P7M67 2011
  577.4'8—dc22                              2010013037

Every effort has been made to contact copyright holders of any material reproduced in this book. Any omissions will be rectified in subsequent printings if notice is given to the publisher.

All the Internet addresses (URLs) given in this book were valid at the time of going to press. However, due to the dynamic nature of the Internet, some addresses may have changed, or sites may have changed or ceased to exist since publication. While the author and publisher regret any inconvenience this may cause readers, no responsibility for any such changes can be accepted by either the author or the publisher.

# About this Book

The introductory pages of this book describe the world's biomes and then the tropical grassland biome. The five main chapters look at aspects of tropical grasslands: climate, plants, animals, people, and the future. Between the chapters are detailed maps that focus on key grassland regions. The map pages are shown in the contents in italics, *like this*. Exclamation-point icons on the map pages draw attention to regions where the biome or its wildlife is under threat. Throughout the book you'll also find boxed stories or fact files about tropical grasslands. The icons here show what the boxes are about. Words in **bold** throughout the book are explained in the glossary at the end of the book. After the glossary is a list of books and websites for further research and an index, allowing you to locate subjects anywhere in the book.

Climate
People
Plants
Future
Animals
Facts
Extinction
Under Threat

# Contents

# BIOMES OF THE WORLD

Biologists divide the living world into major zones named biomes. Each biome has its own distinctive climate, plants, and animals.

If you were to walk all the way from the north of Canada to the Amazon **rain forest**, you'd notice the wilderness changing dramatically along the way (see route marked on map at right).

Northern Canada is a freezing and barren place without trees, where only tiny brownish-green plants can survive in the icy ground. But trudge south for long enough and you enter a magical world of conifer forests, where moose, caribou, and wolves live. After several weeks, the conifers disappear, and you reach the grass-covered prairies of the central United States. The farther south you go, the drier the land gets and the hotter the sunshine feels, until you find yourself hiking through a cactus-filled **desert**. But once you reach southern Mexico, the cacti start to disappear, and strange **tropical** trees begin to take their place. Here, the muggy air is filled with the calls of exotic birds and the drone of tropical insects. Finally, in Colombia you cross the Andes mountain range—whose chilly peaks remind you a little of your starting point—and descend into the dense, swampy jungles of the Amazon rain forest.

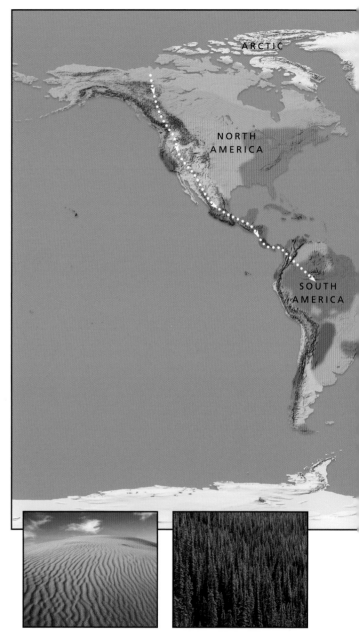

Desert is the driest biome. There are hot deserts and cold ones.

Taiga is made up of conifer trees that can survive freezing winters.

Scientists have a special name for the different regions—such as desert, tropical rain forest, and prairie—that you'd pass through on such a journey. They call them **biomes**. Everywhere on Earth can be classified as being in one biome or another, and the same biome often appears in lots of

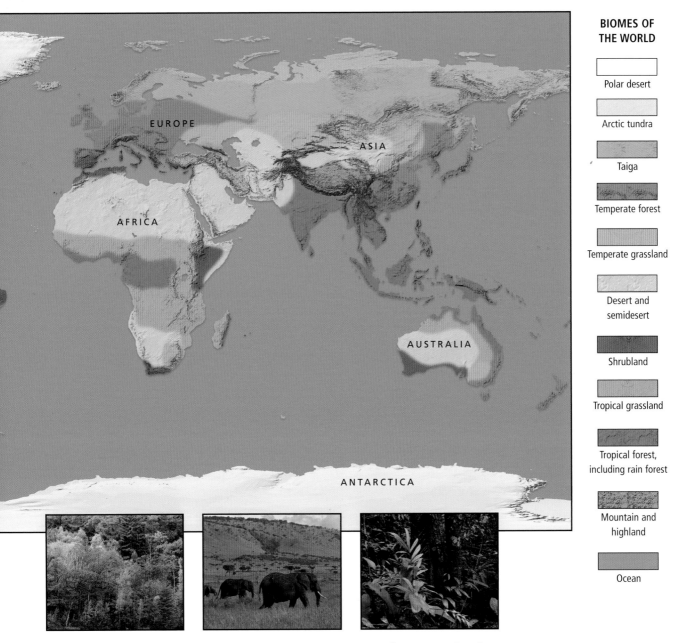

## BIOMES OF THE WORLD

- Polar desert
- Arctic tundra
- Taiga
- Temperate forest
- Temperate grassland
- Desert and semidesert
- Shrubland
- Tropical grassland
- Tropical forest, including rain forest
- Mountain and highland
- Ocean

EUROPE

ASIA

AFRICA

AUSTRALIA

ANTARCTICA

*Temperate forest includes trees that lose their leaves in fall.*

*Tropical grassland, or savanna, is home to the biggest land animals.*

*Rain forest contains the richest mix of plants and animals on the planet.*

different places. For instance, there are areas of rain forest as far apart as Brazil, Africa, and Southeast Asia. Although the plants and animals that inhabit these forests are different, they live in similar ways. Likewise, the prairies of North America are part of the grassland biome, which also occurs in China, Australia, and Argentina. Wherever there are grasslands, there are grazing animals that feed on the grass, as well as large carnivores that hunt and kill the **grazers**.

The map on this page shows how the world's major biomes fit together to make up the biosphere—the zone of life on Earth.

# EARTH'S TROPICAL GRASSLANDS

About 40 percent of the land in Earth's tropical zone is covered by grass or a mix of grass and other plants. Such areas form the tropical grassland biome.

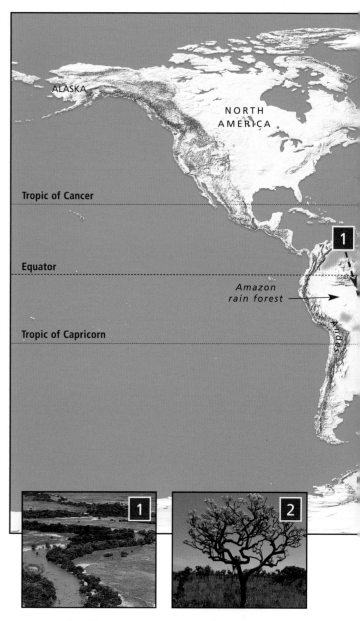

Venezuela's llanos grasslands are riddled with forest-lined rivers.

A lot of Brazil's cerrado savanna has been turned into farmland.

Earth's tropical zone is the area between the **tropics of Cancer** and **Capricorn**—two imaginary circles drawn around the planet 2,600 kilometers (1,600 miles) north and south of the **equator**. In parts of the tropics that are too dry for forest but too wet for desert or **shrubland**, grasslands thrive.

**Tropical grasslands** often have a scattering of trees, forming a landscape termed **savanna**. Most areas of tropical grassland are like this, so the terms savanna and tropical grassland are often used interchangeably. Where the trees get close enough to form a closed **canopy**, the grass disappears and the savanna merges into the **tropical forest** biome.

The biggest area of tropical grassland is in Africa, where flat-topped trees called acacias dot the plains. Africa's savannas are home to gigantic plant-eaters such as elephants and giraffes, vast herds of grass-eating antelope, and some of the world's most dangerous carnivores, including lions and hyenas.

South America has two large areas of tropical grassland: the llanos and the cerrado. Both are mainly savanna, but instead of acacias there are palms or short, gnarled trees. Surprisingly, there are few large animals that live only in the grasslands of South America—most also live in the neighboring tropical forests or shrublands.

Cattle in the dry Sahel of Africa outcompete wild grazing animals.

Hyenas and other large carnivores prowl the savannas of East Africa.

Some people still live off wild foods in northern Australia's grasslands.

In the savannas of northern Australia, **eucalyptus** trees take the place of acacias, and kangaroos replace antelope. Australia's savanna forms a transition zone between the forests of the north and the central desert. As you travel south across it, the forest thins out and gives way to grassland, which in turn peters out into desert.

The map above shows the biggest areas of tropical grassland, but there are also small patches of tropical grassland mixed in with other biomes. There are even patches of savanna in the heart of the Amazon rain forest. Some people also consider most of India to be a kind of artificial savanna, formed long ago by **deforestation**.

# LLANOS

Stretching across northern South America is a huge lowland plain filled with a mixture of wetlands and grasslands—the llanos.

*The skills of the llanos's cowboys, or llaneros, are useful when hunting capybaras, the giant rodents of the area. Capybara meat is salted, dried, and eaten during Easter.*

## Giant Anteater

The llanos are home to more than their fair share of giants, including giant snakes (anacondas) and giant rodents (capybaras). But perhaps the most spectacular is the giant anteater, which looks all the larger for its enormous bushy tail and disproportionately long snout. Giant anteaters are fussy eaters, feeding exclusively on ants and termites. After using their sharp front claws to dig a hole into an ant or termite nest, they poke their long, toothless snout inside and gather prey with a sticky tongue.

The tongue can extend up to 61 centimeters (24 inches) and flicks in and out up to three times a second, gathering grubs and pupae as well as adults. Giant anteaters walk on their knuckles, keeping their front claws curved inward so they don't dig into the ground. They are solitary animals, though youngsters ride on their mothers' backs for up to a year after birth.

## 1. Andes Mountains
This chain of mountains on the west of South America marks the western limit of the llanos. Mountain glaciers are shrinking because of global warming.

## 2. Caribbean Coast
Grassland gives way to hilly shrubland and tropical dry forest along the northern coast of Venezuela. Moist forest flourishes on the mountains.

## 3. Llanos de Apure
An almost treeless flooded savanna in the center of the llanos, home to roseate spoonbills, anacondas, and many other wetland animals. Areas have been drained to make farmland. Oil exploration has caused contamination of parts of the wetland.

## 4. Aguaro-Guariquito National Park
A 612,750-hectare (1.5-million-acre) government-protected area of savanna and wetland, inhabited by anteaters, jaguars, pumas, and capybaras. Poaching is a problem in the park.

## 5. Orinoco River
The main river draining the llanos. Its western tributaries include the Guaviare, Meta, and Apure rivers.

## 6. Orinoco Delta
A complex mosaic of swamp forest, mangroves, and grassland.

In the dry season, agoutis and pacas comb the forest floor for seeds; in the wet season, crocodiles and otters take their place as the delta floods.

## 7. Embalse de Guri
A gigantic reservoir formed in 1986 by construction of a hydroelectric plant on the Caroní River. The dam's reservoir drowned thousands of square kilometers of forest.

## 8. Guiana Highlands
A wild area of highlands, formed from very ancient crystalline rock and covered with savanna and rain forest. Famous for flat-topped mountains called tepuis.

## 9. Angel Falls
The world's highest waterfall, at 979 meters (3,212 feet) tall. The water plunges down the side of a tepui called Devil's Mountain.

## 10. Rupununi Savanna
Distinct from the llanos, this remote area of tropical grassland is surrounded by rain forest. Grass is the dominant plant here because the sandy soil and high ground cannot hold enough water for trees.

## 11. Amazon Basin
The world's largest river basin, mostly filled with dense tropical rain forest. Clearing of forest for logging and to make farmland is a global concern.

## Fact File

▲ The llanos lie between the Andes mountains, the Caribbean Sea, and the Guiana Highlands. Their total area is about 570,000 square kilometers (220,000 square miles)—about the area of Texas.

▲ There are various threats to the llanos: drainage of its wetlands to create fields for crops or livestock, pollution of the wetlands by farmland pesticides and fertilizers, and damming of rivers, which affects the natural flooding cycles of the llanos.

▲ The llanos receive more rain than most tropical grasslands. Rainfall varies from 1,000 millimeters (39 inches) in the east to 4,570 millimeters (180 inches) near the Andes. The dry season lasts 5–6 months in the east but only 1–2 months in the southwest.

# GRASSLAND CLIMATE

Tropical grasslands mostly occur in warm countries with marked wet and dry seasons. However, there are many factors besides climate that influence where tropical grasslands grow.

*Right: The Sun sets over the savanna of East Africa. Day turns to night surprisingly quickly near the equator, the Sun sinking straight down at about 6 P.M. every day.*

## After the Dinosaurs

Tropical grassland is one of the youngest biomes. During the age of the dinosaurs, there was no such thing as grassland because grass plants hadn't evolved. Plant-eating dinosaurs probably ate ferns, conifer trees, and palmlike plants called cycads.

Scientists know from fossil evidence that land plants first appeared about 450 million years ago, and grass—a type of flowering plant—appeared about 50 million years ago. However, it was another 30 million or so years before savannas formed, starting in South America. In the last 20 million years, Earth's climate has become cooler and drier. As a result, the lush forests that once covered the tropics have shrunk, and tropical grasslands have expanded in their place.

In the rain forest of central Africa, the weather is hot and humid all year round. Winter doesn't exist, and the Sun rises and sets at about the same time every day of the year. Travel north to the Sahara desert, though, and things are different. Instead of cloudy skies and frequent downpours, the sky is a flawless blue, and it almost never rains. In summer it is unbearably hot—even in the middle of the night—but in winter the nights can be bitterly cold.

The African rain forest and the Sahara desert both have their own distinctive pattern of weather through the year, which we call their **climate**. The rain forest has a constantly wet climate, the desert a constantly dry one. The climate of tropical grasslands is typically a mixture of the two: soaking wet for half the year and bone-dry for the rest.

## The Tropical Zone

Climates are caused by the uneven way that sunlight warms our planet. Earth spins like a top as it orbits the Sun, staying roughly upright. The **equator** faces the Sun directly, so it basks in strong sunshine every day of the year. The poles, on the other hand, get very little warmth. What sunlight they receive is spread over a wide area because of Earth's curved shape, making the Sun's rays feeble. It's a bit like shining a flashlight on a wall: If you hold the flashlight at an angle, the beam spreads out and casts a weaker light.

Tropical grasslands are in the zone of warm weather near the equator, where the Sun's rays are most intense. They are part of Earth's tropical zone—the region between the tropics of Capricorn and Cancer, two imaginary circles on either side of the equator. Outside the tropics is Earth's **temperate** zone, where the weather is cooler.

Land in the tropics receives about five times more heat and energy per square kilometer than in the far north and south, so it isn't surprising the climate is much warmer. The average daytime temperature in tropical grasslands is usually more than 24°C (75°F), and it doesn't vary a great deal through the year. The steady, warm temperature gives plants and animals a great advantage over the wildlife of temperate grasslands, since they never have to deal with freezing winter weather. And the endless, intense sunshine makes plants grow quickly.

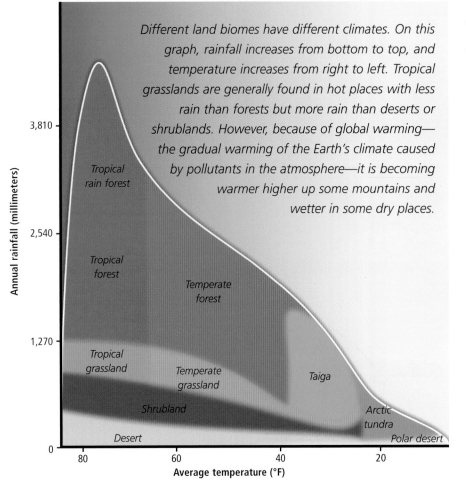

*Different land biomes have different climates. On this graph, rainfall increases from bottom to top, and temperature increases from right to left. Tropical grasslands are generally found in hot places with less rain than forests but more rain than deserts or shrublands. However, because of global warming—the gradual warming of the Earth's climate caused by pollutants in the atmosphere—it is becoming warmer higher up some mountains and wetter in some dry places.*

**Annual rainfall (millimeters)**

3,810

2,540

1,270

0

Tropical rain forest

Tropical forest

Temperate forest

Tropical grassland

Temperate grassland

Taiga

Shrubland

Arctic tundra

Desert

Polar desert

80 · 60 · 40 · 20

**Average temperature (°F)**

## Rain Belt

The Sun's energy doesn't just create warm weather in the tropics—it also produces rain. Sunlight warms the surface of the tropical oceans, filling the air with water vapor and making the weather humid and clammy. Because the air is warm, it rises into the sky, carrying the water vapor with it. As the water vapor rises, it cools, which makes it turn back into liquid and fall as rain. As a result, Earth's equator is surrounded by a belt of warm and rainy weather—the climate that creates tropical rain forests.

The warm air that rises over the equator can't continue rising forever. When it cools high in the **atmosphere**, it stops rising and gets pushed

## Grassland Microclimates

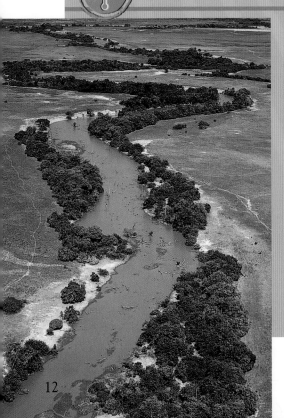

Maps of the world's biomes give the impression that each biome covers a vast area without change, but the truth isn't so simple. Savanna is really a mosaic of forest and grassland, with the number of trees varying from place to place. Trees are most common in rainiest parts of the savanna, and sparse in drier areas. There are even patches of tropical forest right in the middle of the savanna. These grow in areas with an unusual microclimate— weather or conditions different from the surroundings. For instance, wet riversides in the llanos of Venezuela (left) are often covered with trees, forming a habitat termed gallery forest. These strips of forest occur in most tropical grasslands and often contain the same types of trees that grow in tropical rain forests. Likewise, mountaintops are sometimes covered with cloud forests, which thrive on the fog that forms in cold, high air. In East Africa, an enormous volcanic crater called Ngorongoro has cloud forest around the rim but grassland in the center.

away from the equator by the air rising behind it. Now cold and dry, the air begins to fall back down, sinking thousands of miles north and south of the equator. Because it no longer carries water vapor, it causes dry weather where it sinks. The world's major hot deserts, such as the Sahara in northern Africa, exist because of this sinking dry air.

## Wet and Dry Seasons

If Earth stayed completely upright as it orbited the Sun, the belts of equatorial rain and sinking dry air would always be in the same place. But Earth is tipped over slightly, making it spin at an angle, and this is why there are seasons. During summer in the northern **hemisphere**, the North Pole tilts toward the Sun, causing warm, sunny weather and long days. In winter, it tilts away from the Sun, resulting in cold weather and long nights.

Earth's tilt also affects the climate in the tropics, but it produces wet and dry seasons instead of warm and cold ones. When the North Pole tilts toward the Sun, northern parts of the tropics become warmer than southern parts, so the belt of warm, rising air around the equator shifts north slightly, taking the rainy weather with it. For northern parts of the tropics, therefore, July is usually the middle of the rainy season. At the same time, southern parts of the tropics move into the zone of sinking, dry air, resulting in a dry season. In January the opposite happens: Southern parts of the tropics are deluged with rain, while northern areas have a dry season.

Areas close to the equator stay under the belt of rainy weather nearly all year round, creating ideal conditions for tropical forests,

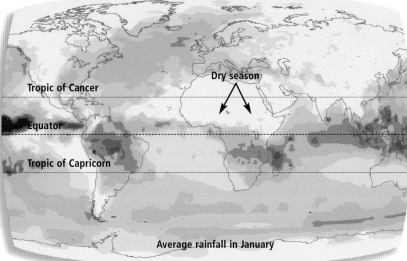

*A belt of rainy weather (blue) surrounds the equator. It moves north in summer (above) and south in winter (below), creating wet and dry seasons.*

but the zones to the north and south of the forests have marked wet and dry seasons. As a result, grasslands are most common in the northern or southern parts of the tropics.

On average, tropical grasslands receive 1,000–1,500 millimeters (40–60 inches) of rain a year. By comparison, deserts receive less than 250 millimeters (10 inches), and rain forests may receive more than 2,500 millimeters (100 inches). However, there are also tropical grasslands in areas with much less or much

*Towering cumulus clouds herald the return of the wet season in Africa's Serengeti grasslands. The hazy region below this cloud is a distant downpour.*

more rain than the average. A more important factor than total rainfall is the length of the dry season, which usually lasts 5–7 months. If the dry season is any longer, the land is more likely to be shrubland or semidesert; any shorter and forest takes over.

The severity of the dry season also matters. Tropical grasslands usually occur where the dry season brings weather as harsh as a desert's. Although some rain may fall, it quickly **evaporates** in the heat, leaving the ground parched and dusty. This harsh weather is stressful for plants, especially trees. In grasslands with a less severe dry season, trees can survive by shedding their leaves or becoming **dormant** (inactive). But in the driest tropical grasslands, only grasses survive.

*Parts of Venezuela's llanos grasslands are flooded in the wet season. The temporary marshes provide perfect cover for giant anacondas—the world's biggest snakes.*

## Monsoons

Some parts of the world have an especially severe wet season called a monsoon. One of the most extreme monsoons occurs in India, which is drenched with rain every year from June through September.

The cause of a monsoon's intensity is the uneven warming of land and sea. Land warms up more quickly under strong sunlight than does the sea, making air rise faster above it. During the northern summer, the vast landmass of Asia heats up. The air over land absorbs this heat and rises, sucking in more air from the Indian Ocean like a giant vacuum cleaner. The air traveling from the ocean (called the monsoon wind) picks up moisture from the sea and dumps it on India as rain.

India's monsoon is so powerful that it draws moisture-bearing wind away from East Africa, creating a dry season in the savannas of East Africa—even though these grasslands lie on the equator, where tropical rain forests would normally prevail.

Even within one area of tropical grassland, the length of the dry season varies from place to place. The wettest places, in which trees are most common, are where the grassland borders tropical forest. As you travel across the grassland toward the desert biome, the dry season gets longer and the trees become sparse. In dry parts of the grassland, the rainy season is not only shorter but also less reliable. In some years, it fails to rain at all.

### Breaking the Rules

Although tropical grasslands generally occur in places with a marked dry season, they often break this rule. There are many patches of tropical grassland mixed in with other biomes, especially tropical forest. There are even patches of tropical grassland in the heart of the Amazon rain forest, where it rains nearly all year round.

The explanation for these rule-breaking patches of biome is that other factors besides climate determine where grasslands grow. One such factor, for instance, is soil type.

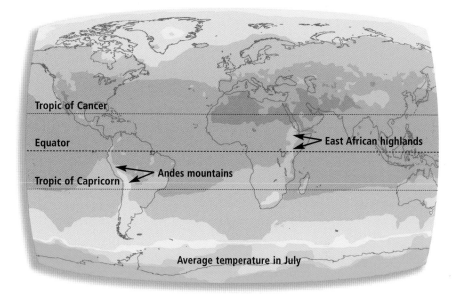

*The tropics stay warm all year round, shown by warm colors (darker shades of orange) on these maps. Mountains are cooler than lowlands.*

## Unreliable Rains

In many parts of the world, people take the seasons for granted. In North America, for instance, winter never fails to arrive, bringing cold weather and long nights. But in the tropics, the seasons are less reliable. The people and animals of tropical grasslands depend on the annual rainy season to bring back the rich grass, but sometimes the rains do not arrive. The result is a drought: The land turns to desert, animals cannot find food and die, crops wither, and people often starve as well.

Some people blame droughts on global warming—the gradual warming of the planet as a result of higher levels of greenhouse gases, such as carbon dioxide, in the atmosphere. Scientists are still unsure of the long-term effects of global warming on grasslands. Some grasslands may become drier, others wetter. However, droughts have always been a natural part of the tropical grassland climate. The risk of drought has had an interesting effect on how the wildlife has evolved. Unlike the animals and plants of tropical forests, those of tropical grasslands tend to have short lives, but they mature quickly and produce more offspring. This means they can quickly recolonize the land after a drought.

# Climographs

Each place in the world has its own pattern of weather, or climate. We can sum up a place's climate on a climograph, such as the one shown here for St. Louis (right). The letters along the bottom are the months of the year. The numbers on the left and the small bars show rainfall, and the numbers on the right and the curvy line show temperature. Unlike St. Louis, most tropical grasslands (below) are hot all year round and have pronounced wet and dry seasons. Nairobi in Kenya has two wet seasons each year.

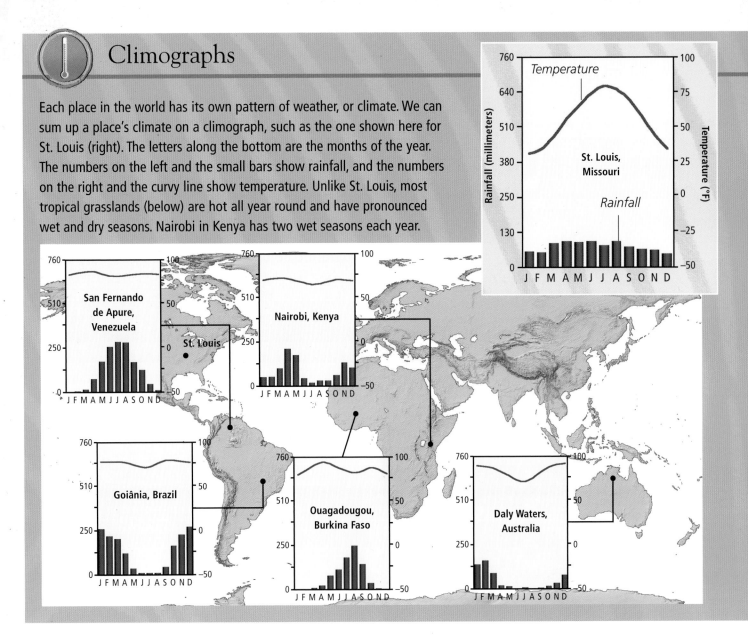

If the soil is too stony for trees, or if water drains through it too easily, grasses will flourish where there would otherwise be forest. The well-drained volcanic soil of the Serengeti in Africa is virtually treeless in places for this reason. Likewise, grass takes over in areas that are so boggy that the soil becomes acidic and low in **nutrients**—many of the patches of grassland in the Amazon rain forest formed this way.

The soil in tropical countries is often red because of an insoluble chemical called iron oxide (rust), which tends to build up over time as the rain washes other chemicals away. Soils that are very rich in iron oxide are called laterites. They tend to bake solid in the tropical sunshine, forming a hardpan below the surface that blocks roots and so stops trees from growing. In the wet season, the hardpan traps water, making the ground too waterlogged for trees. Though some types of palm trees can survive in laterites, the plants that usually dominate are grasses.

## Grassland Fires

Another important factor is fire. Dry grass makes perfect kindling for wildfires in the dry season. Unless animals have nibbled the grass down to the ground, the continuous cover of grass spreads the fire over vast areas. The fire kills tree seedlings, but grass plants survive thanks to underground roots and shoots.

*Mist often hangs over Africa's savannas in the cool early mornings. Lions and other big predators do most of their hunting during the night and around dawn, avoiding the stifling heat of the day.*

Regular fires, therefore, can create grassland where there would otherwise be forest.

Fires start naturally during thunderstorms, which are common toward the end of the dry season. All it takes is a single dry lightning strike to set the land on fire. However, most tropical grassland fires are probably started by people, often deliberately. In the Sahel region of Africa, for instance, people have been burning grassland for more than 2,500 years in order to clear trees and shrubs and thus create better grazing land for livestock. Today, an estimated 75 percent of Africa's tropical grassland is burned each year.

Animals, too, can turn forest into grassland. When grazing animals nibble tree seedlings, they kill the plants by biting off the buds. Grass plants, in contrast, have buds

*Below: These termite mounds in northern Australia are called compass mounds because they always face east and west. This probably helps control the microclimate inside the mounds. During cool early mornings and late evenings, the mounds catch the warmth of the rising and setting Sun, but at midday their thin shape catches much less sunlight, helping prevent overheating.*

*Thunderstorms are common in the tropics, especially at the end of the dry season. If lightning strikes dry grass, it can trigger a wildfire.*

nibble the grass very close to the ground, fires cannot spread; without fires to kill off bigger plants, trees and shrubs begin to take over.

Livestock and people have had such a big influence on tropical grasslands, and for so long, that it is often difficult to say which grasslands are natural or artificial. The truth is that most tropical grasslands are probably seminatural, which means that human activity has been an important part of the biome's ecology for many thousands of years.

at the base of the plant or underground, so they quickly recover from grazing. However, excessive grazing can have the opposite effect, turning grassland into forest. If animals

## Ancient Fires

The Aboriginal people of Australia have probably been setting fire to the savanna since their ancestors arrived on the continent at least 50,000 years ago. While people in other parts of the world use fire to clear land for crops, Aborigines didn't begin farming until very recently. Instead, they used fire to flush animals out of the bush, or to clear scrub to make hunting and traveling easier. Before the arrival of Aborigines, the savanna region of Australia might have been covered with tropical forest. There are still patches of tropical forest in parts of the savanna that fire doesn't reach, such as volcanic crater floors and rocky gullies.

# CERRADO

South and east of the Amazon Basin, the climate is too dry for rain forest. In its place is the cerrado: a largest expanse of tropical grassland.

Cerrado trees (right) look contorted because new growth starts each wet season from side buds.

 Fact File

▲ The cerrado is a mosaic of savanna, shrubland, and dry forest. Dense gallery forests border rivers.

▲ Thick, gnarled bark gives the cerrado's trees protection against fire. In some tree species, up to two-thirds of the trunk's width is bark.

▲ There are at least 10,400 plant species, 180 reptile species, 837 bird species, and 195 mammal species in the cerrado. Many live nowhere else.

## Wolf on Stilts

The maned wolf is the largest member of the dog family native to South America. Although called a wolf, it lives alone rather than in a pack, and it looks more like an elegant fox than a wolf. Its long legs help it peer over tall grass or bushes while hunting. Its prey, which it stalks and then leaps on with a stiff-legged pounce, include armadillos, pacas, rabbits, and birds. However, more than half the maned wolf's diet consists of seasonal fruits, plant roots, and bulbs. In Brazil, some people believe the animal has magical powers, including the ability to kill a chicken with its gaze. The left eye of a live wolf is sometimes cut out and kept as a good luck charm.

**1. Gran Chaco**
A dry shrubland area between the cerrado and the Andes mountains, home to jaguars, pumas, tapirs, giant armadillos, and numerous reptiles. Much of this area has been converted into farmland.

**2. Chapada dos Guimarães National Park**
This protected area lies in the transition zone between the cerrado and the Amazon forest. Colorful toucans and macaws live among the park's cliffs, waterfalls, and gallery forests.

**3. Pantanal**
A marshy depression grazed by cattle in the dry season but flooded in the wet season, leaving only hilltops exposed. The Pantanal is one of the world's largest freshwater wetlands and is a haven for wildlife, although farmland fertilizers and pesticides washing into these wetlands affect aquatic wildlife.

**4. Paraná River**
South America's second longest river after the Amazon flows 4,880 kilometers (3,032 miles) from the Brazilian Highlands to its mouth in the South Atlantic. Parts of the river are polluted.

**5. Itaipu Dam**
One of the largest hydroelectric plants in the world, jointly owned by Paraguay and Brazil. Its construction created a vast reservoir, completely submerging vast areas of forest and the once spectacular Guaíra Falls.

**6. Iguaçú Falls**
A dramatic, horseshoe-shaped waterfall where the Iguaçú River plunges off the Paraná Plateau into a deep gorge. National parks in both Brazil and Argentina protect the rich wildlife around the falls.

**7. Emas National Park**
A protected area of cerrado with a mixture of shrubland, savanna, and open grassland, dotted with brick red termite mounds as tall as a person.

**8. Brasília**
The capital of Brazil, established in the 1950s. In the last 60 years, building and the spread of farming around both Brasília and the new highways serving the city have destroyed large areas of the cerrado.

**9. Brazilian Highlands**
An area of rolling hills, deep valleys, and plateaus, with an average height above sea level of 1,000 meters (3,300 feet).

**10. Caatinga Shrubland**
Almost impenetrable thorny shrubland in the northeast, where the climate is very dry. Poaching threatens wild animals in this shrubland.

# GRASSLAND PLANTS

Grassland plants are among the toughest plants on Earth. They can spring back to life after being starved of rain for months, chewed to stumps by animals, and burned to a crisp.

If you were to visit Africa's Serengeti grasslands twice in one year, you might get a surprise. In May, toward the end of the main rainy season, lush green grass carpets the ground as far as you can see. But in September, in the dry season, things could hardly be more different. What little grass remains has turned to straw, and the dusty ground looks like a desert.

The same thing happens in tropical grasslands in many other places. Every year, a blistering dry season drains the land of color, and the grass shrivels under the relentless tropical Sun. Yet when the rains return, the same desiccated plants somehow spring back to life and turn the landscape green again.

The plants of tropical grasslands spend around half the year living through desert conditions, but that's not the only challenge they face. In the dry season, they have to contend with raging wildfires, fueled by the tinder-dry straw. And in the wet season, herds of grazing animals trample across them and eat them. To most plants, such constant hardship would be lethal. However, grass plants not only survive being maimed, burned, and starved—they thrive on it.

## A World of Grass

The grass family is the success story of the plant world. Since grass plants first evolved a mere 50 million years ago, grasses have spread across the world and taken over vast swaths of land. One reason for their success was a gradual cooling and drying of Earth's climate, which favored drought-tolerant plants. Another reason was the relatively recent appearance of a **species** that has a very special relationship with grasses: humans.

Grasses are able to establish themselves quickly on disturbed land. As humans spread around the world, felling forests and changing the landscape, grasses soon followed them.

 Photosynthesis

Like animals, plants cannot survive without food. Unlike animals, however, they don't have to eat—they can make food. Plants need only a few simple ingredients to make food: water, air, and sunlight. Inside the cells that make up a plant's leaf (right) are tiny food-making factories called chloroplasts. These contain the green substance chlorophyll, which gives plants their color. Chlorophyll captures energy from sunlight and uses it to combine water and carbon dioxide from air into food molecules.

## Bloated Baobabs

The baobab trees of Africa, Madagascar, and northern Australia are expert water storers. During the wet season, they soak up massive amounts of water and store it within soft, spongy wood inside the trunk and lower branches, which swell up like balloons. When the dry season begins, baobabs shed their leaves (which reduces water loss) and slowly draw on their hidden reserves; as the water gets used up, the trunk appears to shrink. Baobabs can cope with very long dry seasons and grow in semideserts as well as savanna. They grow slowly but reach enormous sizes. One hollow tree in Zimbabwe is large enough for up to 40 people to shelter inside its trunk. Other baobabs have been used as a shop, a prison, a house, and a bus shelter.

*Tall grass makes a good hiding place for small animals, such as this klipspringer, a type of antelope from Africa.*

Grasses are the botanical equivalent of rats—wherever people live, you're sure to find grasses thriving in patches of wasteland and in nooks and crannies among buildings. But grasses are not just weeds—for thousands of years, humans have deliberately bred and grown grasses for their edible seeds. Cereal crops such as wheat, rice, and corn, which together form the staple foods for most people on Earth, are the descendants of wild grasses. The seed heads of these plants have become grotesquely enlarged by years of careful breeding—known as selective breeding—so much so that they hardly look like grasses anymore.

The properties that make grasses successful weeds also equip them for life in tropical grasslands. The harsh dry season, regular fires, and hordes of grass-eating animals continually disturb the land, just as human settlements disturb natural habitats. Grasses have evolved all sorts of features that overcome the constant trauma.

## Topsy-Turvy Plants

Have you ever mowed a lawn and wondered why the grass plants don't die when you cut them? In most plants, the growing parts (called meristems) are at the top, or inside buds next to branches. If you cut the stalk, you remove all the growing parts and the plant dies. Grasses are different: Their growing parts are at the bottom instead of the top. When you mow a lawn, all you do is cut through the blades of grass, leaving behind the growing parts. New blades soon spring up.

The unusual position of the meristems helps grass survive constant munching by animals. In fact, grazing animals can help grass plants. Although they damage the grass blades, the grazers do more damage to other plants growing nearby. In the process,

*Despite lacking front teeth, white rhinos nibble grass right to the ground with their lips. Yet grasses can survive even this drastic pruning.*

## Jeepers Creepers

Africa's tropical grasses are aggressive plants—so much so that they are taking over other parts of the world. Scientists have found that some parts of tropical America, where forests had been removed for agriculture, are now covered with such African grasses as paragrass, pangola grass, and jaragua. In southern parts of the United States, one of the most common grasses in lawns and golf courses is Bermuda grass (right), an African savanna species that spreads by growing creepers (horizontal stems). Oddly enough, American grasses introduced into Africa have not had anything like the same success.

they clear the ground of competition, allowing the grasses to dominate. Mowing a lawn has the same effect: It kills most weeds and so creates a turf of pure grass.

Some savanna grasses respond to grazing by growing faster—the more that animals nibble the grass, the quicker it grows back. In fact, certain

grass species can't survive without being grazed. One example is an African grass called *Andropogon greenwayi*, which makes up about half the grass in parts of the savanna that are regularly grazed. When people put up fences to keep animals away, *Andropogon greenwayi* disappears and other plants take its place.

## Threats to Plants

The plants of tropical grasslands are adapted to tough conditions, but they face several threats. Introduced plants species are a particular problem. These are plants brought into a region by humans, often grown as crops or garden plants. Many spread into the wild and outcompete native plants for nutrients and water. Native plant-eating animals, or herbivores, often cannot eat these plants. Invasive plants include the African grass jaragua in the South American llanos and blue gum trees in parts of the African savanna. In addition, global warming and overgrazing by domestic livestock are threatening the survival of many tropical-grassland plants.

Having a continuous haircut is no problem for grass plants, so they have little need for thorns or poisons to ward off animals. As a result, tropical grasslands are a living banquet —vast herds of plant-eating animals can gorge themselves on the fast-growing grasses, which soon grow back. In contrast, plants in tropical rain forests defend themselves against **herbivores** with an armory of chemical weapons, such as tannin (which makes leaves indigestible) and strychnine (a lethal neurotoxin). Rain-forest animals have to be much more choosy about what they eat.

## Going Underground

During the dry season, the blades and flowers of most tropical grasses wither, dry out, and die. But the grass plants themselves do not die—they store their food reserves underground in swollen roots or stems, which

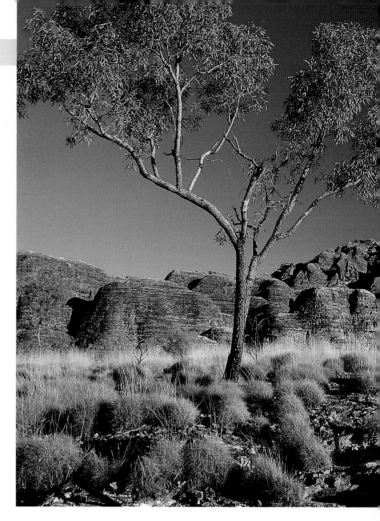

*Above: The tussock grasses (bunch grasses) of northern Australia grow in large clumps called tussocks, giving the ground a lumpy appearance.*

*Flame lilies get through Africa's dry season by storing food in an underground swelling termed a tuber. They bloom in the wet season, using long, twining leaves to crawl up through the grass and reach the light.*

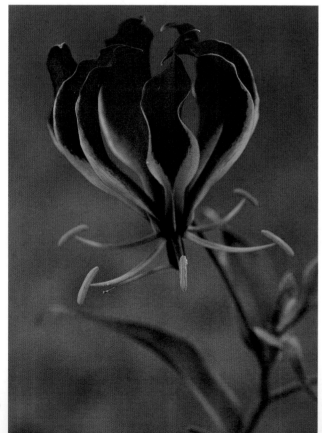

stay inactive until the next wet season. These underground parts have tiny buds, ready to sprout into action when the rains return. Other tropical grassland plants, such as orchids and lilies, use the same trick. Like hibernating animals, all these plants survive the harsh weather by conserving their energy, doing very little, and hiding. In West African savannas, the total weight of plant matter underground may be up to four times as much as that above the surface. All this hidden material provides food for armies of burrowing animals, especially termites, worms, and rodents.

Not all grasses stop growing in the dry season, though. Some species continue growing, but much more slowly. These grasses are common in places that have occasional

## Pointless Pollen

Like other flowering plants, grasses produce flowers, which allow them to reproduce sexually. The male parts of flowers make a windblown dust called pollen, while the female parts produce sticky receptors to catch pollen. When pollen lands on the female part of a flower, the male and female sex cells join and a seed forms. Or at least that's what usually happens—but some grasses have abandoned the sexual process. They still go to the trouble of producing flowers and pollen, but instead of reproducing sexually they clone themselves at the last minute, making seeds that grow into carbon copies of the single parent.

Scientists think the grasses that reproduce this way do so because it preserves a very successful combination of genes. When organisms reproduce sexually, genes from the parents mix together. This results in varied offspring, each with a unique set of genes and unique strengths. However, it also scrambles the parental genes like decks of cards being shuffled, breaking up useful combinations.

*Below: Madagascar is home to the bizarre elephant's-foot plant, so named because its bloated stem looks like a severed elephant's foot that has sprouted flowers.*

bursts of rain in the middle of the dry season. By keeping a few tiny shoots alive above ground, they are ready to spring to life before other plants when conditions improve.

Remaining underground is not just a good way of surviving dry weather—it's also an excellent defense against the wildfires that sweep across tropical grasslands every dry season. Like grazing, fire can help grass plants. For one thing, it kills tree seedlings, stopping them from growing big enough to shade out the grass. It also clears the ground of debris, allowing new shoots to emerge into full sunlight as soon as they break the surface.

## Year after Year

In temperate countries, such as North America, many plants are **annuals**. Annual plants don't try to survive the harsh winters. Instead, they simply die after scattering their seeds and leave the seeds to grow into new plants the next year.

In tropical grasslands, there are very few annual plants. Most are **perennials**—plants that carry on growing year after year. Perennials have one big advantage over annuals: By storing food reserves, they can spring to life more quickly in the growing season. In contrast, plants that grow from seeds start off small and take weeks to grow large. When the wet season begins, there is a race to grow as quickly as possible to colonize the bare ground. Perennials are quickest. Helped by the warmth and the intense sunshine, they cover the ground in days. Late starters risk being left in the shade, without enough sunlight to grow properly.

Another strategy that helps grass plants take over quickly is the way they reproduce. Although tropical grasses can reproduce by seed, they rely much more on cloning themselves. Instead of growing upward, some

*Acacia trees develop a flat canopy because giraffes and other animals nibble them from below.*

Equator

Percentage of land
covered by trees:

More than 45

30–45

15–30

10–15

5–10

Not grassland

## Woodland or Grassland?

Books about Africa's savannas sometimes call them woodland, dry forest, bush, or scrub instead of grassland. The reason for all the confusion is that savanna is really a mixture of trees and grass, with the number and height of trees varying from place to place.

This map shows how the density of trees varies across all of Africa's grasslands (including grassy areas of desert and shrubland). Toward the center of Africa, where the climate grows wetter, trees get increasingly dense until they merge into rain forests. Farther from the equator, where the climate is drier, the trees thin out until there is little but grass.

grass stems creep along the ground or grow horizontally under the surface. At a certain distance, these stems take root and produce a new tuft of shoots. The resulting clumps of grass, called tussocks, are a common sight in most tropical grasslands. This way of reproducing is much faster than making seeds and allows a single plant to colonize a large area quickly with clones of itself.

## Flat Tops and Twisted Trunks

Most tropical grasslands have at least a scattering of trees and shrubs as well as grasses. The trees are most abundant in the rainiest areas or where the soil is damp, and they gradually thin out as the grassland merges into desert or shrubland. There are also occasional thickets, especially along river banks or near water holes.

In Africa and Madagascar, most of the trees in savannas are acacias—members of the same family of plants as peas and beans. Like their relatives, acacias produce nutritious

seedpods that are full of **protein**, and much sought after by giraffes, elephants, and antelope. But the seeds themselves are not always fully digested. When they pass out of the animal, they land on the ground in a heap of dung, which provides the perfect fertilizer. So, in a way, the trees pay the animals to spread their seeds and plant them.

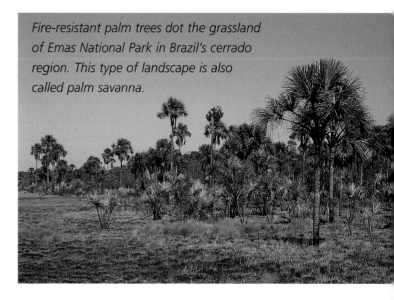

*Fire-resistant palm trees dot the grassland of Emas National Park in Brazil's cerrado region. This type of landscape is also called palm savanna.*

# The Whistling Thorn Tree

If you stand next to an acacia tree in the savannas of East Africa, you might hear it whistling. The noise comes from the wind blowing through holes in swellings at the base of thorns (right), which act like tiny flutes. Thanks to the tree's musical ability, people call it the whistling thorn tree. The swollen thorns provide homes for particularly aggressive types of ants, the acacia ants. In addition to housing the ants, the tree produces sugary secretions that feed them. In return, the ants protect the tree from animals. When a giraffe tries to grab a mouthful of leaves with its tongue, the ants swarm out of their thorns and attack with vicious stings.

As young acacias grow, their sides tend to get nibbled by animals, but the center of the plant, where the leaves and pods are out of reach, grows tall. Once this part of the tree has become too tall for even giraffes to reach, it spreads out, giving the tree its famous flat-topped appearance.

Savanna trees have to contend with the same problems as grasses—the long dry season, unpredictable rain, wildfires, and hungry animals—but they overcome these problems in different ways. The baobab tree gets through the dry season by absorbing as much water as it can in the wet season and swelling in size. It also sheds its leaves and stays bare for up to nine months a year.

With deeper roots than grasses, trees can reach farther underground for water. One Brazilian savanna tree has roots that grow up to 18 meters (60 feet) deep. Being able to reach deep water allows savanna trees to keep growing in the dry season, and even to flower. To conserve water, such trees often have small, leathery leaves, with fewer pores than other trees. The eucalyptus trees of Australia look like this. They are called evergreen trees because they always have leaves. However, many savanna trees shed their leaves when the dry season begins and wait for the rains to return—they are called deciduous trees.

Most savanna trees are shorter than their forest cousins, with a more twisted shape. This is especially true of Brazil's cerrado, which is dotted with what look like gnarled and stunted little apple trees. The trees grow this way because new twigs and branches

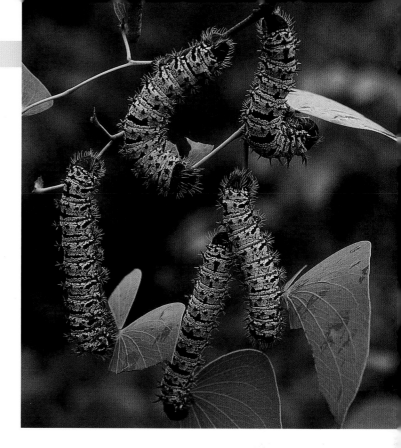

*One of the most common trees in the savannas of Zimbabwe and Botswana is the mopane tree. In the wet season its distinctive, butterfly-shaped leaves are devoured by caterpillars called mopane worms, which local people harvest for their nutty flavor.*

develop each wet season, sprouting from buds hidden under the bark. In the driest parts of the cerrado, the same plant species are so gnarled and stunted that they form shrubs rather than trees.

Fire is less of a problem for tall trees than for grasses because their buds and leaves are out of the flames' reach. Nevertheless, savanna trees generally have thick, corky bark that protects the living tissue below from being scorched. If an intense fire burns through the bark, many trees can produce new sprouts from their roots or stumps. Of all savanna trees, the masters at surviving fire

*The punishing climate makes the trees of Brazil's cerrado grow into grotesque shapes. The fruits of this monkey-nut tree look and taste like those of its close relative the cashew-nut tree.*

are the eucalyptus trees of Australia, which can sprout up from the ground year after year despite being completely burned down.

Tropical grasslands are full of life, but they are tough places to survive in. As a result, the plants do not live as long as in tropical forests. Except for baobabs, which can live thousands of years, very few shrubs or trees last more than a few decades. The same is true of grassland animals. They lead short and stressful lives, and must contend not only with fires and droughts, but also with some of the world's deadliest **predators**.

 ## What a Sucker

The eucalyptus's apparently miraculous ability to survive being burned is due to its unusual roots. Many eucalyptus trees have large root swellings called lignotubers, as well as a network of underground branches called suckers. After a fire, the tree draws on the food stored in its lignotubers and quickly produces new shoots from the suckers, which emerge from the ash-covered ground.

# SAHEL AND SUDANIAN SAVANNA

To the south of Africa's mighty Sahara desert is a vast belt of mostly dry tropical grassland. It forms a transition zone between sandy desert to the north and forest to the south.

*Many of the Sahel's people live by traveling with cattle herds in search of fresh pasture, a way of life called nomadic pastoralism.*

### 1. Djoudj National Bird Sanctuary
This wetland in the Senegal River Delta is a sanctuary for more than a million birds, including white pelicans, purple herons, African spoonbills, and great egrets.

### 2. Senegal River
A west-flowing river on the Senegal–Mauritania border. It floods in the wet season, creating huge wetlands that many migrating birds visit. The floods also nourish rich pasture, providing precious grazing for people's livestock.

Pollution by fertilizers is a problem in the river.

### 3. Inland Niger Delta
A region of lakes and creeks formed where water from the Niger River fills wind-eroded depressions in the ground. The region dries out in droughts or severe dry seasons. Overfishing, the spread of farmland, and dams threaten the balance of nature in the delta.

### 4. Niger River
Western Africa's principal river. It flows in a great arc

## Fact File

▲ The Sahel is a semiarid region of grassland bordering the Sahara. The Sudanian savanna is a more lush grassland to the south of the Sahel.

▲ Only tough, drought-resistant plants, such as tussock grass and shrubby acacia trees, survive in the Sahel. Taller acacias, elephant grass, and combretum trees flourish in the Sudanian savanna.

▲ The dry season lasts 8–9 months in the Sahel and 5–7 months in the Sudanian savanna. Grasses wither and trees shed their leaves during the dry season.

▲ Climate experts are unsure how global warming will change Africa's savanna. Some think it will become drier; others think it will become wetter.

through the Sahel and Sudanian savanna and meets the Atlantic Ocean at the Niger Delta.

## 5. Chad Basin National Park
Migrating birds, ostriches, gazelles, and giraffes are among the residents of this reserve in Nigeria.

## 6. Waza National Park
Cameroon's most famous national park hosts more than 1,000 elephants—the largest concentration of the animals in the Sahel and Sudanian region. Poaching is a problem in the park.

## 7. Lake Chad
This shallow freshwater lake has been shrinking for thousands of years. In recent decades, droughts have reduced the lake's area dramatically and turned the land around it to desert. Lake Chad is a vital source of freshwater to both people and wildlife.

## 8. Sahara
An enormous sandy desert that takes up almost all of northern Africa. The desert is expanding southward because of overgrazing of livestock and, possibly, global warming.

## 9. Manovo-Gounda St. Floris National Park
The best-protected area of savanna in the Central African Republic, once home to rare African hunting dogs and critically endangered black rhinos. Armed poachers have killed many of the animals and have made the park too dangerous for tourists.

## 10. White Nile
One of the two main tributaries of the Nile, Africa's longest river. The swamp-fringed White Nile flows through Sudan before joining the Blue Nile at Khartoum, the capital of Sudan. Parts of the river are polluted by oil.

## 11. Ethiopian Highlands
Savanna merges into lush mountain grasslands and tropical forests in the highlands of Ethiopia, home of the rare Ethiopian wolf.

AFRICA

# Clinging On

The Sahel and Sudanian savanna does not have such rich wildlife as East Africa's savanna. One reason for the difference is the drier climate, especially in the north, which makes it difficult for all but the toughest animals to survive. Another factor is hunting. In the 20th century, hunters equipped with rifles and four-wheel-drive cars killed off many animals that were once widespread here, such as lions and cheetahs. A third factor is disease—or rather the lack of it. In East and Central Africa, a disease spread by the tsetse fly made livestock farming difficult until recently, but the drier parts of northern Africa are free of the tsetse fly. As a result, herders have long been able to drive their cattle across the grasslands, causing inevitable conflict with wild animals. Even so, populations of elephants, giraffes, and other animals, such as chameleons (below), survive in parts of the Sudano-Sahelian savanna, especially in government-protected reserves.

# GRASSLAND ANIMALS

For animals, grasslands are one of the richest biomes on Earth, with food covering the ground for kilometers on end. Yet life here is anything but easy—the animals must struggle constantly not only to find their next meal but to avoid becoming someone else's.

*African elephants use their vast ears as radiators to help them lose heat. They also flap their ears wide open as a sign of anger.*

*Trunks have more uses than Swiss army knives. Elephants use them for smelling and touching objects, tearing up grass, stripping bark and leaves off trees, squirting water, throwing dust, and scratching itchy skin. They also serve as trumpets for making sound and as snorkels for breathing underwater.*

##  Weaver Birds

Grass has other uses besides being food. Mice use it to line their nests, and lions use it for cover while stalking prey, for instance. But perhaps the most imaginative use of grass is that shown by weaver birds. Members of this bird family weave strips of leaves and grass into elaborate nests high in savanna trees. Hanging upside down by their feet, they use their tiny beaks to knot the strips together with incredible dexterity. Some species even add a trumpet-shaped entrance tube. In southern Africa, sociable weavers transform trees into huge colonies, with hundreds of nests joined together. Only the males build nests. The females select their partners by the quality of their craftsmanship.

Tropical grasslands are home to the biggest and most spectacular land animals on Earth. In a brief drive across Kenya's Masai Mara National Reserve, it takes a matter of minutes to spot elephants, giraffes, lions, hippos, and cheetahs, not to mention vast herds of zebras and wildebeest, and a handful of different gazelle species. Most of these animals belong to a group that scientists call ungulates—the hoofed **mammals**.

### On the Hoof

An ungulate is an animal that has hooves and eats plants. Ungulates dominate many of the world's grasslands, both temperate and tropical, because they are experts at digesting grass. For many animals, humans included, grass is a poor quality food. Its cells have a tough outer coating made of a substance called cellulose, which is tricky to digest. Many grasses also contain crystals of silica (sand), which scratch an animal's teeth and wear them down. Ungulates have several ways of getting around these problems.

The teeth and jaws of ungulates work like grinders, crushing grass so powerfully that the cells split open, releasing the nutrients inside. Powerful cheek muscles move the lower jaw sideways, scraping the flat-topped teeth across each other to mash up the grass caught in between. Silica is no problem because ungulate teeth have huge crowns that continually grow as they wear away.

The digestive system of most ungulates contains billions of cellulose-digesting bacteria. In some ungulates, including wildebeest and gazelles, these bacteria live in a stomach chamber called a rumen; such animals are called **ruminants**. Swallowed food sits in the rumen for up to four days while the bacteria get to work on it. Then the animal brings the rotting grass back up to its mouth to chew it a second time. Ruminants have a very efficient digestive system, but it works

## Strange Diets

Although ungulates are basically plant eaters, a few sometimes eat animals to supplement their diet. Small antelope, such as duikers, eat birds when they can catch them. Warthogs—ugly relatives of farmyard pigs—eat insects, birds, mice, frogs, worms, beetles, rotten meat, and elephant dung, as well as plant food. Giraffes often eat bones (above) left by scavengers, though doing so occasionally gives them fatal food poisoning.

slowly and they can't take in huge amounts of food. As a result, such animals are fussy about what plants they eat, choosing only the youngest, most nutritious shoots.

Other ungulates have cellulose-digesting bacteria in the rear part of their digestive system. Zebras, elephants, and rhinoceroses all digest food this way. It's quicker but less efficient than rumination, so they have to take in more food to compensate. These animals can survive on the tougher or older bits of grass, but they have to eat huge amounts of it. Elephants can even eat bark.

### Living Together

One of the reasons that many different ungulate species can coexist in a savanna is that they feed on different types of plant matter. In Africa, zebras and wildebeest often

*Left: Impalas are ruminants, preferring the most tender grasses and herbs. The elegant, lyre-shaped horns of this animal identify him as a male.*

live in mixed herds. While the zebras feed on the rough tops of grass plants, the wildebeest eat the small shoots that the zebras have exposed. It doesn't always work out so fairly, however. Wildebeest are often followed by small, nimble gazelles that use their narrow muzzles to steal the shoots uncovered where the ground is trampled. Rather than shooing these intruders away, the wildebeest simply move on to where the grazing is better.

*Herbivores can be just as violent as carnivores, especially when fighting over mates. Male plains zebras kick and bite each other viciously in their battles over females.*

Some ungulates are browsers rather than grazers: Instead of eating grass, they nibble leaves or berries from the savanna trees. As with grazers, different browsers prefer different bits of the same tree. Giraffes browse among the highest branches, using their incredibly long and flexible tongue to reach between thorns and pluck off leaves. Long-necked antelope called gerenuks stand on their back legs to reach medium-height leaves, while small antelope such as dik-diks browse near ground level. Because trees have much deeper roots than grass, they can reach deeper water and continue growing in the dry season. This is an advantage for browsers. While grazers have to move away in the dry season to search for fresh pasture, browsers can stay put. They even survive in drier places such as shrublands and deserts.

## Moving On

One of the biggest challenges that grassland animals face is the dry season. Browsers can get by on shrubs and trees, but grazers are not so lucky—their main source of food shrivels up and disappears. In South America, white-tailed deer and pampas deer stay near water holes or rivers, surviving on a mixture of grazing and browsing. They live in small herds, which makes the food last longer. In northern Australia, wallabies and kangaroos also survive on a mixed diet. Rather than forming herds, they spread out and live singly, again reducing competition for food. In Africa, however, there are vast herds of animals that eat only grass. They have no option but to migrate.

## A Life of Danger

Grassland herbivores live a life of constant danger—especially in East Africa, where they share the savannas with many of the world's deadliest carnivores. To survive, the herbivores need ways of giving the predators a run for their money.

One defensive strategy is speed. Most ungulates are quick on their feet, especially antelope, gazelles, and zebras, which can reach speeds of 64–80 km/h (40–50 mph). Even a newborn antelope can get to its feet and run within about 15 minutes of birth. The fastest savanna ungulates can outrun most predators, though they cannot match the speed of their temperate-grassland cousins the saiga and pronghorn, among the fastest land animals on Earth. Some antelope also try to confuse their pursuers by dodging randomly or making sudden, stiff-legged leaps into the air while running. The springbok earned its name from its spectacular defensive leaps, which can reach 3.5 meters (11.5 feet) high. Australia's largest native herbivores—kangaroos—also use speed to escape predators. Large kangaroos can sustain hopping speeds of more than 56 km/h (35 mph), using their heavy tails to stay balanced and aid sudden maneuvers.

## Big Is Best

Another strategy is size. Elephants, buffalo, and rhinos are too big for most predators to overpower, though their young are much less safe. Large animals are likely to stand their ground rather than flee when threatened, and many can charge at attackers with alarming speed and ferocity. Giraffes also gain some protection from size, but lions can bring them down by driving them into broken ground where they are likely to trip. Despite their ungainly stature, giraffes can run at 56 km/h (35 mph), though their graceful strides give the appearance of moving in slow motion.

# The Migration

One of the world's most spectacular natural events is the migration of wildebeest in East Africa—biologists simply call it "the migration." Every year, herds of up to 1.5 million wildebeest leave the southeast of the Serengeti National Park in Tanzania as the dry season begins. Accompanied by zebras and gazelles, they travel northwest toward Lake Victoria, then north into Kenya's Masai Mara National Reserve, where there is permanent water and lush grass. They face many dangers on this perilous journey, such as river crossings where hundreds fall prey to crocodiles. When the rains return, the wildebeest head south again, braving the rivers once more to return to their starting point. Savanna animals also migrate in other parts of Africa, though on a smaller scale. In the west of Africa's Sahel grasslands, for instance, elephant herds travel in a giant circle that takes in wetlands and lakes when the dry season is at its worst.

There is something puzzling about the great migrations in Africa. In the Masai Mara, there is good grazing all year round, so why don't the animals simply stay put? Scientists have not yet solved this mystery, but there seem to be several factors involved. One is the large number of big cats and hyenas in the Masai Mara. These big predators tend to stay in one territory rather than migrate, because their babies cannot walk easily (unlike baby wildebeest and elephants, which can walk within hours of birth). So although the Masai Mara has good grazing, the danger of being killed by a predator there is much higher. Another factor is food quality. The grass in the Masai Mara contains very little of the mineral phosphorus, which is vital for healthy bones. During the dry season, the wildebeest develop a phosphorus deficiency, but this disappears when they return to the mineral-rich grasslands in the southeast of the Serengeti.

Lake Victoria

KENYA

Mara River

August–November (dry season)

Masai Mara

N

Wildebeest migration route (cream)

Park boundary (red)

June–July (transitional)

Gurumeti River

Serengeti National Park

TANZANIA

December –May (wet season)

Ngorongoro Crater

Park boundary

Migration route

AFRICA

0        50 miles
0        50 kilometers

## Swarming Locusts

Just like wildebeest, some plant-eating insects make mass migrations to find fresh grazing. Certain types of locusts form swarms so vast that they can look like dust storms. A single swarm may contain as many as 10 billion locusts—enough to strip farmland bare in a matter of minutes, causing a famine.

Locusts are normally solitary insects, colored green or yellow for camouflage. But if they become crowded together and their food runs out, something strange happens. They lay eggs as normal, but the hatchlings grow into large-winged, black-and-yellow locusts that cluster together before flying off in a swarm. Most swarms form on the dry fringes of the savanna, where the rains are unreliable and the food supply erratic. In 2004, swarms of locusts devastated crops in northern and western Africa. Loss of harvests led to food shortages in many countries. The estimated cost of the damage was about three billion US dollars.

## Safety in Numbers

Animals that live in herds, flocks, or family groups benefit from safety in numbers. With so many eyes and ears on the alert for danger, predators find it much harder to sneak up and take them by surprise. Gazelles warn one another of danger by flashing their white tails and leaping. Like many herbivores, but unlike most predators, they have eyes positioned on the sides of the head. This arrangement gives a very wide field of view, the better to spot an approaching predator. Meerkats take turns keeping a lookout, perched on a bush or rock, while the rest of the group forage about on the ground for food. If danger threatens, the lookout barks a noisy warning, sending the whole group scurrying for cover.

## Seeking Sanctuary

Burrows provide a relatively safe haven for all sorts of small grassland animals, especially rodents, such as mice and rats. Their underground homes not only provide a hiding place from predators but also protect them from the sweltering midday heat of the dry season or the torrential rain of the wet season. In the llanos of Venezuela, cane mice emerge from their burrows at night to feast on grass seeds. In good years, they explode in number and wear down conspicuous runways through the grass. In Africa, naked mole rats spend their entire lives underground, feeding on roots, **bulbs**, and other plant parts. Their social groups are unique among mammals—each colony has a queen that bears all the young, while the other mole rats are workers.

The baboons and patas monkeys of Africa (among the few **primates** that live in grassland rather than forest) spend the night sleeping in trees or on rocky cliffs, where most predators

*Small herbivores rely on speed to outrun cheetahs, but youngsters such as this Thomson's gazelle are often too slow or clumsy to escape.*

*Hopping might look ungainly, but gray kangaroos can reach speeds of 56 km/h (35 mph)—nearly twice as fast as a person can sprint.*

cannot reach them. At sunrise they come down to forage for food on the ground. Like most monkeys, they have excellent color vision for finding food in daylight, but very poor night vision. In contrast, big herbivores such as zebras, which have no choice but to spend their nights on the open plains, have good night vision. They stay awake most of the night, watching nervously for lions and hyenas, which are most active in the hours of darkness. Like horses, zebras sleep in short bursts while standing up, their leg muscles locked in place to prevent their falling over.

## A Taste for Flesh

Where herbivores are common, carnivores are never far away. The savannas of East Africa are famous for the wide range of flesh eaters they harbor, from big cats and hyenas to vultures and birds of prey. Less spectacular, but equally important, are the insect eaters that thrive on the countless ants, termites, caterpillars, and grasshoppers. In South

*Meerkats give warning calls to their group when they spot predators. They use a special call for birds of prey, telling the group to sprint headlong to the nearest hole.*

*Long-nosed armadillos eat insects and other small animals. Oddly, their litters always consist of genetically identical offspring—like identical twins.*

*Pangolins specialize in eating ants and termites. Like armadillos, they can curl up into an armored ball to defend themselves against predators.*

America these include armadillos and giant anteaters, while pangolins and aardvarks play similar ecological roles in Africa.

Animal flesh is a very nutritious type of food—much more so than grass—but predators have to work hard to get it. Grassland herbivores are nervous and quick-witted animals, liable to bolt at the first sign

*Only by working together can lions overpower animals as large as adult buffalo. A powerful bite to the throat quickly kills the animal.*

of danger, and tough enough to put up a serious fight. To catch them, predators need cunning, strength, speed, and perseverance.

## Working Together

Some hunters use teamwork to trap or overpower their prey. Prides of lions spread out during the hunt, using any cover available to creep within striking distance before making an attack. When their prey tries to escape, a few lions often stay hidden, ready to ambush animals that blunder past.

Wildebeest and zebras are among their favorite prey when lions hunt in packs, while solitary lions often kill warthogs. However, like many carnivores, lions are opportunists, willing to tackle all sorts of prey (including people) in many different situations, as well as scavenge the kills of other predators.

Hyenas are best known as scavengers, but the largest species—the spotted hyena—is also a pack hunter, able to bring down zebras and even buffalo. Spotted hyenas are also called laughing hyenas because of the eerie cackles and "wooooo-up" calls they make to one another. They are attracted by the sound of commotion and use their sharp sense of smell to sniff out carcasses. Packs of hyenas often muscle in on leopards or cheetahs after a hunt, using strength of numbers to steal the kill. Leopards drag kills into trees to avoid this fate, while cheetahs hunt mainly during the day, when hyenas are usually resting.

*Above: Spotted hyenas have immensely powerful teeth and jaws. They can crush and eat all but the largest bones and chew their way though thick hides.*

 ## Cheetahs

Very few cheetahs survived the last ice age, which ended about 10,000 years ago. Therefore, all the cheetahs around today—in Africa and the Middle East—are descended from the same few ice-age survivors. A long period of inbreeding followed this "bottleneck," which has resulted in today's cheetahs having a low level of genetic variation. This is a risk to the survival of the species, especially when it comes to susceptibility to disease. For example, if an infectious disease—such as a strain of flu—develops that could overcome the immune system of one individual cheetah it would overcome the immune systems of all other cheetahs, too.

## Clean-Up Squad

Contrary to popular belief, African vultures do not rely on leftovers from predator kills. They feed mainly on the carcasses of animals that die of sickness or old age. Typically, white-headed vultures find a carcass before any other vultures do. But soon hoards of griffon vultures such as the white-backed vulture (above) arrive, squabbling noisily. Their bald heads let them plunge deep into a carcass and come out clean. Eventually, huge lappet-faced vultures arrive to muscle their way in. It takes only a day or so for a carcass to disappear from Africa's savanna, thanks to the work of nature's clean-up squad.

## Lone Hunters

Leopards and cheetahs usually hunt alone, using different strategies to catch their prey. Leopards hunt by stealth, hiding in trees or thickets to sneak close enough to ambush antelope and other prey. Cheetahs use speed to run down small gazelles and antelope in daylight, favoring young animals, which are slower and less nimble than adults. After

Unlike the big cats, which generally bring down prey after a sudden dash, African hunting dogs chase their victims over long distances, gradually wearing them out. Small animals are torn apart and devoured in a frenzy as soon as they are caught; larger animals are often disemboweled during the chase by repeated bites to the flank and rear. Once common in Africa's savannas, hunting dogs are now very rare, possibly because of diseases spread by domestic dogs.

*Ground hornbills of the African savanna are fearsome hunters. They catch snakes, frogs, and small mammals.*

*Dingoes are the top predators in Australia's grasslands. Though wild today, they are descendants of tame dogs brought to Australia by people thousands of years ago.*

tripping the prey with a flick of the paw, the cheetah kills it with a suffocating bite to the neck—a technique common to all cats. Cheetahs are the fastest animals on land, capable of about 100 km/h (60 mph) on level ground, but they can sprint for only 10–30 seconds before they risk overheating.

## Around the World

To most people, the word *savanna* conjures up images of vast herds of hoofed mammals roaming over grassy plains, ever watchful for lions, hyenas, and other big predators. In East Africa, that's a fairly accurate image, but not all tropical grasslands are like that. Compared to the savannas of Africa, South America's tropical grasslands seem almost devoid of large animals. Africa has around 91 different ungulate species, but South America has just 21, and only three of those live primarily in tropical grasslands. Australia has no native ungulates. Instead, wallabies and kangaroos are the main plant eaters in the savanna.

The reasons for these differences are complicated. According to evidence from fossils, South America's grasslands may once have been as rich in animal life as Africa's, but about 10,000 years ago many of the animals disappeared. No one knows exactly why. Perhaps people hunted them to extinction, or perhaps the climate changed and the animals couldn't adapt. Whatever the reason, the animals that were left behind were much less diverse. Today, most of the mammals that live in the llanos and cerrado are the same species that live in South America's tropical forests. There are exceptions—such as the maned wolf, a kind of dog that looks like a fox on stilts, and the pampas deer—but they are few.

 Gone Forever

Until about 4,000 years ago, Australia had its own native version of a big cat: the thylacine, or Tasmanian tiger. This marsupial stood about 60 centimeters (2 feet) at the shoulder and looked like a mixture of other animals: It had the head and front legs of a wolf, hind legs more like a kangaroo's, and a striped back. Competition with dingoes probably led to thylacines dying out in Australia, but they survived on the island of Tasmania until the 20th century. Sadly, they were hunted to extinction by sheep farmers; the last captive animal died in 1936.

*Ostriches (left), rheas (center), and emus (right) live in different parts of the world but have similar grassland lifestyles. These males are all guarding nests.*

Australia's story is different. The mammals of Africa, Asia, and the Americas are similar because these continents were joined until about 175 million years ago and species spread between the continents. South America once had elephants, for instance, and its jaguar is a close cousin of Africa's big cats. Australia, however, has been separate from the rest of the world for much longer, cut adrift with a unique collection of **marsupials** (mammals with pouches). Another difference is that Australia has no large predators, apart from the ones that people have introduced. The nearest thing to a lion in Australia is the dingo—a wild dog descended from tame dogs brought to Australia by Aborigines.

Despite the differences, there are some striking similarities in the animal life of the world's major tropical grasslands. One similarity is the presence of large flightless birds: ostriches in Africa, emus in Australia, and rheas in South America. All three have lost the power of flight and have long, powerful legs for sprinting across the open terrain; ostriches can reach 60 km/h (37 mph) when just a month old.

Ostriches, rheas, and emus share some surprisingly similar patterns of behavior.

In all three species, the male mates with several females, incubates their eggs in a communal nest, and looks after the young when they hatch. All three species live in flocks for protection from predators, and their diets are similar, consisting mainly of plants and seeds and supplemented by insects such as grasshoppers. Ostriches—the world's largest birds—also eat lizards and turtles.

Just why these birds are so similar is a matter of hot debate. Some scientists think they evolved along similar lines because they live in similar environments—a process termed convergent evolution. However, other scientists think the birds inherited these traits from a common ancestor that lived millions of years ago, when Earth's continents were joined in one landmass.

## Grassland Insects

Another similarity among the world's tropical grasslands is their insect life. The biggest grass-eaters in savannas are mammals, but the animals that eat the most grass are much smaller. Hordes of grasshoppers and ants scurry and hop through the turf, while caterpillars munch the leaves and armies of termites collect dead plant litter.

*Termite mounds provide handy lookout towers for baboons and other animals. Deep inside, the grotesquely enlarged queen (inset) is busy laying eggs.*

# Dung Beetles

Dung beetles clear up fresh manure from tropical grasslands almost as fast as it appears. Working quickly while the dung is still soft and pliable, they form it into balls and roll these away to their burrows. Once safely underground, the beetles lay eggs in the dung balls, and the grubs develop inside them. Some dung beetles don't go to the trouble of making dung balls and rolling them away; instead they dig a burrow right under the main dung heap. One Australian species does not even dig burrows—it has evolved into a parasite that lives in the large intestines of wallabies.

Termites play the role of recyclers. They consume a quarter to a third of the dead plant matter in tropical grasslands, though they don't always eat this directly. The fungus-growing termites carry litter deep into their complex nests and use it to grow fungi, which members of the colony then eat. Like ants, termites are social insects. A colony may contain many thousands of individuals, but all the eggs are laid by a single queen. A queen termite can lay thousands of eggs a day and grow as large as a person's finger— so large that she is unable to move. In many savannas, the termites build spectacular, towering mounds that dot the landscape, forming so-called termite savannas. Within the mound, the temperature and humidity are remarkably constant, providing the perfect environment for the fungus garden and developing termite larvae.

# EAST AFRICA

East Africa's savannas are famous for their astonishing diversity of large mammals and for the spectacular mass migrations of wildebeest and zebras.

*Mount Kilimanjaro's snowcapped peak dominates the skyline over Kenya's Amboseli National Park.*

 ## Ngorongoro Crater

Ngorongoro Crater is one of the wonders of the natural world. Packed into this 20-kilometer-wide (12-mile-wide) volcanic crater is just about every large mammal species to be found in East Africa's savannas, including lions, hyenas, elephants, wildebeest, zebras, and rhinos. The crater even has hippo-filled water holes and its own soda lake, complete with thousands of pink flamingos. Many of the animals stay year round, but others come only in the dry season, attracted by permanent water on the crater floor. Even without wildlife, Ngorongoro would be amazing. Surrounding the central grassy plain is a 600-meter-high (2,000-foot-high) crater wall, covered in cloud forest. Visitors drive up and over the jungly rim before descending into the sunbaked interior.

## Fact File

▲ Most of East Africa is savanna, but there are also large areas of treeless grassland, shrubland, tropical forest, mountains, and lakes.

▲ There are two rainy seasons in East Africa: a long one between March and June, and a shorter one between October and December.

▲ Kenya and Tanzania rely heavily on income from tourists visiting their national parks. Kenya alone has more than 30 national parks and reserves.

▲ Poaching nearly wiped out East Africa's elephant and rhino populations in the 20th century. Even today, antipoaching patrols in some parks are authorized to shoot and kill poachers.

SUDAN

ETHIOPIA

Lake Turkana

UGANDA

KENYA

SOMALIA

N

**8** ⊙
Mount Kenya

Equator

⊙
**3**
Lake Victoria

Masai Mara Reserve

**5** ⊙

● Nairobi

Amboseli National Park

Tsavo National Park

RWANDA

**4**
Serengeti National Park

⊙ **10**

**11**

BURUNDI

**6**
Olduvai Gorge

Kilimanjaro ▲

**9**

Lake Tanganyika

**7** ⊙
Ngorongoro Crater

● Mombasa

**2** ⊙

TANZANIA

Indian Ocean

DEMOCRATIC REPUBLIC OF THE CONGO

Pemba Island

Zanzibar Island

**1**

**1**

0    200 miles
0    200 kilometers

● Dodoma

● Dar es Salaam

Rift Valley

### 1. Great Rift Valley
A massive depression in Earth's surface, formed by gradual separation of the African and Arabian landmasses. It extends all the way from Jordan in southwest Asia to Mozambique in Africa, where its east and west branches average 48–64 kilometers (30–40 miles) wide.

### 2. Lake Tanganyika
In the western branch of the Great Rift Valley is the world's longest freshwater lake. It is also the world's second deepest lake. Overfishing has depleted stocks of fish in the lake.

### 3. Lake Victoria
The world's second largest lake, and Africa's largest, occupies a shallow basin between the two branches of the Great Rift Valley. The region around Lake Victoria is one of the most densely populated parts of Africa. Extinction of fish species, pollution, and invasive water hyacinths are problems in the lake.

### 4. Serengeti National Park
Tanzania's most famous national park, some 15,000 square kilometers (6,000 square miles) in area. Its almost treeless grassy plains are home to millions of wildebeest and zebras.

### 5. Masai Mara National Reserve
This Kenyan reserve is joined to Tanzania's Serengeti. Packed with lions, it is one of Africa's top tourist attractions. A slump in tourism in 2007–2009 led to an increase in the poaching of wildlife.

### 6. Olduvai Gorge
An archeological site in the Serengeti plains where footprints and fossils of ancient hominids (ancestors of the human race) have been found.

### 7. Ngorongoro Crater
A massive volcanic crater in Tanzania, rich in savanna wildlife and rimmed by cloud forest. Protected as a world heritage site, a biosphere reserve, and a Tanzanian national park. There are no rhinos in the crater and hunting dogs have recently disappeared.

### 8. Mount Kenya
An extinct volcano in the Kenyan highlands, 5,199 meters (17,058 feet) high, where giant lobelias, groundsel trees, and other unusual plants grow. Illegal logging threatens this area.

### 9. Kilimanjaro
At 5,895 meters (19,340 feet), this extinct volcano is Africa's highest mountain and one of the only places in Africa that gets snow.

### 10. Amboseli National Park
Kenya's second most popular park after the Masai Mara. Huge herds of elephants survive here, but poachers have wiped out all the rhinos.

### 11. Tsavo National Park
Kenya's largest national park, at around 20,000 square kilometers (8,000 square miles) in area. The region was once home to the "Tsavo man eaters," a pair of male lions that ate about 35 railroad workers in 1898.

# PEOPLE AND GRASSLANDS

Tropical grasslands were the cradle of our species and shaped our evolution. Today the relationship is reversed—we are reshaping the world's biomes and changing tropical grasslands beyond recognition.

In 1976, the **paleontologist** Andrew Hill made a remarkable discovery at Laetoli in the Serengeti plains of Tanzania. After a long day of fossil hunting, Hill and his colleagues were amusing themselves by flinging elephant dung at one another. As Hill dived onto the ground to avoid a particularly well-aimed lump, he found himself staring at fossilized animal tracks on the ground. The discovery was a major breakthrough, but it was nothing compared to what Hill's colleagues found under the footprints. When geochemist Paul Abell quarried out a section of rhino tracks, he saw two new sets of prints underneath. These footprints, some 3.6 million years old, were unmistakably the tracks of a pair of **hominids**—apes that walked on two legs, just as humans do.

## Origins

The Laetoli footprints are one of the oldest pieces of evidence suggesting that our two-legged ancestors originated in the savannas of Africa, perhaps four or five million years ago.

*The 3.6-million-year-old Laetoli footprints were made by two hominids walking side by side. A third individual also seems to have walked in the larger footprints.*

Today, humans are the only members of the great ape family that walk on two legs habitually. Chimps and gibbons occasionally stand and walk a few paces, but the skill has limited use in their forest habitats. Hominids, in contrast, evolved the ability to stride for miles across a more open landscape. Their legs became straighter, their toes shrank, and their skulls changed shape to balance on an upright spine.

The evolution of two-legged walking, or bipedalism, seems to have been linked to a change in the African environment. About five million years ago, savannas were spreading throughout tropical Africa because Earth's climate was growing cooler and drier.

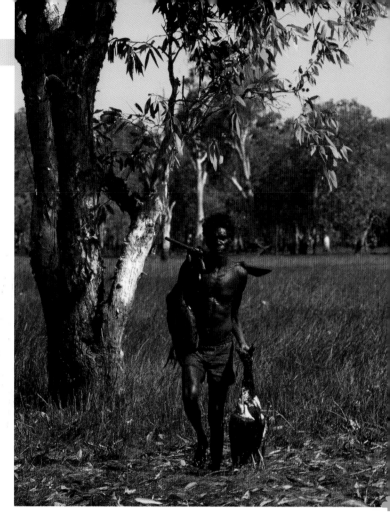

*The Aborigines of northern Australia harvest food from the wild, a way of life termed hunter-gathering. Unlike hunter-gatherers in rain forests or deserts, however, they also use fire to manage the savanna landscape.*

As the forests dwindled in size, our tree-dwelling ancestors evolved better ways of getting about on the ground.

In addition to evolving a new posture, hominids lost most of the body hair that had covered their apelike predecessors, and they evolved a far more efficient sweating system. These two changes allowed hominids to stay active during the heat of the day in the open savanna environment, exposed to tropical sunshine. The price they paid for their advanced cooling system was a continual need for water—our ancestors probably never strayed very far from rivers or water holes.

Adjusting to life on the savanna not only affected our ancestors' bodies, it also changed their diet. Forest foods such as fruit and nuts became harder to find, while roots, grass seed, and meat became more important. Having no natural weapons for killing large prey, the early hominids probably got much of their meat by scavenging in groups. However, with their hands free to make tools, they soon began making hunting weapons, such as simple knives made from chipped rocks and spears made from sharpened sticks.

Humans have now spread throughout the world's biomes, yet we retain our tropical biology. Instead of evolving blubber or fur in colder climates, for instance, we built houses and made clothes to re-create a tropical microclimate. One of the few evolutionary changes caused by our spread to new biomes was the development of paler skin, helping us to make vitamin D in weak sunlight.

## Two Legs or Four?

Why tree-dwelling apes should evolve into two-legged (bipedal) rather than four-legged walkers is a matter of debate. After all, other savanna primates, such as baboons and patas monkeys, manage perfectly well on all fours. Some scientists think bipedalism evolved because the upright posture exposed less of the body to midday sunshine, helping hominids avoid overheating when out in the open. Others think the main advantage was the ability to look over the grass and scan the horizon for predators or prey. Or, perhaps, bipedalism enabled our ancestors to carry their offspring and so follow the herds of migrating herbivores—something other predators, such as lions, cannot do. Whatever the reason, bipedalism had a very important consequence: It freed the hominids' hands, allowing them to make and use tools.

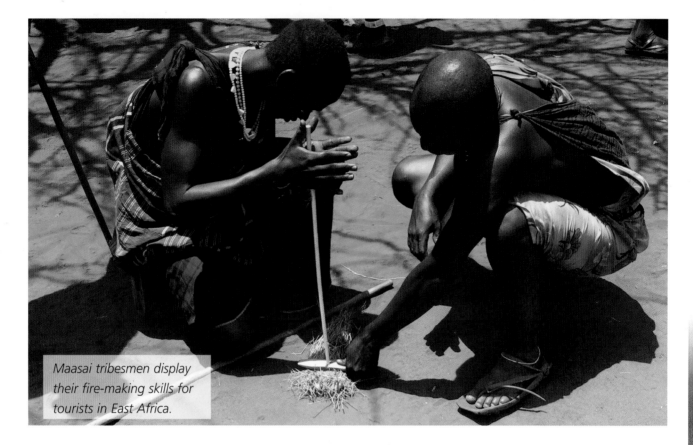

Maasai tribesmen display their fire-making skills for tourists in East Africa.

## The Modern World

Human culture has changed beyond recognition since our hominid ancestors first conquered the savanna. The development of language, greater intelligence, and complex societies have had such far-reaching consequences that all the world's people now live in very different ways from our ancestors. However, we can get clues about how people may have lived in the distant past from the way some modern people survive in tropical grasslands, using only natural resources and knowledge handed down over the generations.

## Hunter-Gatherers

Before the spread of agriculture and the domestication of animals, most of the world's people were **hunter-gatherers**—they lived off food collected from the wild. Today, very few people live as hunter-gatherers in tropical grasslands, but one exception is the Aboriginal people of Australia.

The Aborigines' way of life is changing fast, but many still collect wild foods in remote parts of Australia, including the tropical grasslands of the north. The bulk of their diet comes from plant foods, such as wild roots and grass seeds, which women grind into flour. Insect grubs and other small animals provide a valuable source of protein, supplemented by meat from larger animals caught in traps or hunted. A traditional hunting technique is the use of fire to smoke out wallabies and other large prey from thickets. Native mammals were never kept as livestock, probably because, unlike cattle or goats, marsupials do not usually form herds.

Despite the apparent simplicity of their hunter-gatherer lifestyle, Aborigines manage the landscape in a careful and deliberate manner, using fire to clear scrub and keep the savanna open. In recent times, European ranchers have claimed much of Australia's savanna for their cattle, and fires are now much less frequent. As a result, woody vegetation has begun to reclaim the land, turning the ancient savanna into forest.

The relationship between fire, people, and grasslands is an ancient one. People have lived in tropical grasslands for millennia and used fire for just as long. Many savannas that we consider wild are probably seminatural, like the savannas of Australia.

## Nomads and Herders

In contrast to the Aborigines, the savanna-dwelling peoples of Africa live mostly by traveling with herds of animals, a way of life called nomadic pastoralism. Just as wild herbivores must migrate across the savanna

away in the dry season. Besides providing meat, their animals provide milk or blood—renewable sources of food and liquid that can be taken without killing the animals.

In southern parts of the Sudanian savanna, people grow crops as well as herd animals. However, in the drier Sahel to the north, the rains are not sufficiently reliable for crop cultivation—the only way to survive off the land is by nomadic pastoralism.

Raising livestock, especially cattle, is the main form of land use in savannas throughout the world. In South America, Australia, and parts of Africa, cattle ranching has grown into a major industry, turning what was once wild and diverse savanna

*Cattle ranching is the main form of land use in Venezuela's llanos grasslands. Once a year, cowboys round up the cattle and drive them to rodeos to be sold.*

in search of recent rains and fresh grazing, so pastoralists must stay on the move to keep their cattle fed. The Fulani people of West Africa travel constantly and never settle down. The Maasai people of East Africa have permanent homes but take their herds far

into uniform pasture. The llanos are now home to an estimated 15 million cattle. Ranchers burn the grasslands regularly to release nutrients and clear trees, resulting in deforestation of woodland areas and gallery forest. Though fire has always played a part in savanna ecology, scientists believe its use is on the increase in many parts of the world, with damaging effects on the wildlife.

Cultivation of crops is also on the increase in savannas, though the harsh dry season makes this more difficult than ranching.

## Desertification

In recent decades, a combination of factors have made life very hard for people in the Sahel (below). Governments have tried to make people settle down in one place because of disputes over land, but this has made it difficult for once-nomadic herders to keep their animals properly fed. At the same time, a succession of droughts has reduced the amount of grazing available and forced people to gather around wells. In areas where people are concentrated, grasses soon disappear as the animals eat them, and trees are felled for firewood or fodder. The land becomes barren and dusty, as though swallowed by the desert. Desertification is not confined to the Sahel—it is a problem in other arid places, and many people fear that it will become worse with global warming.

In wet parts of the llanos, hundreds of thousands of acres of grassland have been converted to corn and rice plantations. In recent years, Brazil's cerrado has undergone an even more remarkable transformation as vast plantations of soybeans, corn, and irrigated rice have appeared.

*Soybean fields near Goiás, central Brazil. Irrigated crops such as this one have taken the place of wild savannas throughout much of the cerrado.*

## People Versus Animals

The impact of people on savanna wildlife is nowhere clearer than in Africa. Famous for its fearsome predators and giant herbivores, Africa's savanna is now mostly devoid of large wild mammals, except for pockets of land protected as national parks. This fragmentation of animal populations impacts on their survival because they become inbred, which increases their susceptibilily to diseases and genetic disorders. Outside the parks, the human population is growing, roads and towns are dividing the landscape into islands of wilderness, and domestic herds are replacing wild ones. Tropical diseases that affect cattle (such as trypanosomiasis, which is spread by tsetse flies) have been eradicated from many areas, allowing pastoralists to encroach on untamed parts of the savanna. In other parts, livestock diseases, such as anthrax, have spread to wild animals.

Inevitably, people and wild animals come into conflict. Livestock eat the same plants as wild herbivores, competing with them for food. And herders must protect their stock— as well as themselves—from predators, by whatever means necessary; in some parts of Africa, killing a lion is still regarded as a test of manhood. The 20th century also saw a disturbing rise in poaching, especially of elephants for ivory and rhinos for their horns.

Despite the pressures confronting Africa's wildlife, the future is not entirely bleak. Many conservation projects have been launched, involving local people, in protecting plants and animals. These projects aim to strike a balance between the traditional needs of the people living there and the needs of wildlife. In addition, in recent times, people have begun to realize that one good way to protect wildlife is to make money from it, and a new industry is on the rise: ecotourism.

## Rhino Poaching

After 1970, Africa's black rhino population plummeted from an estimated 100,000 to fewer than 2,500. That makes it critically endangered. The cause of the decline is poaching. Rhino horn is a prized ingredient in traditional Chinese medicines for impotence, and it is in even more demand in Yemen and Oman, where daggers with rhino horn handles are worn by men as a status symbol. With the fall in rhino numbers, the value of their horns on the black market soared from $16 per pound to more than $1,000, making poaching all the more lucrative. Today, nearly all Africa's remaining black rhinos live in fenced reserves with armed guards, and many are dehorned for their own protection (above).

# NORTHERN AUSTRALIA

Savanna covers a great area of northern Australia, sandwiched between tropical forests in the north and desert in the continent's interior.

 Fact File

▲ Trees in Australia's savanna include eucalyptuses, acacias, baobabs, and kakadu plum trees.

▲ Eucalyptus species such as Darwin's woolybutt and Darwin's stringybark are often hollowed out by termites. Australians use the hollow branches to make musical instruments called didgeridoos.

▲ Tree cover decreases from north to south with the increasingly dry climate.

▲ Resident marsupials include kangaroos, wallaroos, wallabies, bilbies, quolls, and long-tailed planigales—the world's smallest marsupials.

▲ The main grass in wet areas is monsoon tallgrass. Drier areas are dominated by Mitchell grass, which grows in tussocks. A Mitchell grass plant can live for 30 years.

▲ Much of the Australian savanna has been cleared for farmland. In addition, introduced plants and animals outcompete the native wildlife.

0              300 miles

0        300       kilometers

Indian Ocean    Eighty-Mile Beach   WESTERN

AUSTRALIA

*Above: Bungle Bungle Range rocks were formed by sediment settling in layers millions of years ago. Forces beneath Earth's crust then lifted the rocks, as wind and water wore them down into these shapes.*

**1. Kimberley Plateau**
A rugged sandstone plateau, covered by savanna and dissected by numerous gorges and ridges. Torrential rains in the wet season fill temporary rivers, causing flash floods. Introduced cane toads threaten the survival of native frogs.

**2. Bungle Bungle Range**
A magnificent range of rocky hills that resemble giant, striped beehives.

**3. Tanami Desert**
Grasslands peter out in this arid part of the outback, leaving sandy plains with scattered clumps of spinifex grass and saltbush shrubs. Native lizards are threatened by feral cats and foxes.

**4. Cattle Ranches**
Cattle ranching is the main form of land use in northern Australia's grasslands. The cattle compete with native animals for grazing and water.

**5. Arnhem Land**
A largely unspoiled wilderness containing eucalyptus forest, savanna, and patches of rain forest and wetland. Arnhem Land provides a refuge for the black wallaroo, the smallest kangaroo in the world.

**6. Barkly Tableland**
A region of rolling grassy hills used as pasture by cattle ranchers.

**7. Gulf of Carpentaria**
Surrounding this enormous bay is a mixture of woody savanna, eucalyptus forest, sandstone cliffs, and saline flats. The region is battered by monsoon rains every summer.

**8. Cape York Peninsula**
Australia's northernmost tip, sparsely populated except for Aboriginal reserves on the coast and cattle ranches. Its native wildlife is threatened by feral pigs and invasive plants.

**9. Queensland Rain Forest**
A small strip of dense tropical rain forest flourishes on the wet coast of Queensland. Plans to mine tin threaten areas of the rain forest.

**10. Great Basalt Wall**
A unique rock feature in the Queensland highlands, formed by a lava flow. Walls of basalt rock surround pockets of savanna. Cattle cannot climb the wall to reach the savanna, so native wildlife can graze without competing with livestock.

PAPUA NEW GUINEA

Timor Sea

Arafura Sea

Melville
Island

Darwin

Kakadu
National Park

*Arnhem Land*

Nitmiluk
National Park

**5**

**7**

Cape
York
Peninsula

Gulf of
Carpentaria

ASIA

AUSTRALIA

N

**1** **!**

Kimberley
Plateau

**!** **8**

Queensland rain forest

Cairns

**9**

**!**

**2**

*C a t t l e r a n c h e s*

Lawn Hill
National Park

Staaten River
National Park

Bungle Bungle Range

**4** **!**

*Barkly Tableland*

Forty Mile Scrub
National Park

Townsville

Coral
Sea

Great Barrier Reef

**!** **3**

*Tanami
Desert*

**6**

*Cattle ranches*

**4**

**10**

Great
Basalt
Wall

Great Dividing Range

NORTHERN

TERRITORY

QUEENSLAND

*Simpson
Desert*

*ranches*

**4**

Rockhampton

# A U S T R A L I A

Uluru-Kata Tjuta
National Park

*Sturt
Desert*

*Great
Victoria
Desert*

SOUTH

AUSTRALIA

*Lake
Eyre*

*Great
Artesian
Basin*

*Darling
Downs*

Brisbane

Gold Coast

*Nullarbor Plain*

*Flinders Range*

*Darling River*

NEW SOUTH WALES

 ## Life in the Pouch

Marsupials raise their offspring in a very different way from other mammals. A mother kangaroo gives birth when its baby is about 1 centimeter (0.4 inches) long. The newborn youngster is blind, furless, and has no hind legs. Using its relatively strong forelimbs, it climbs through the mother's fur and into a pouch, where it stays for up to 11 months, suckling on a teat. After several weeks in the pouch, the young kangaroo (called a joey) is big enough to peer outside and hop out from time to time.

# THE FUTURE

The world's tropical grasslands will continue changing in the future, and much of their wildlife may die out. Yet the grasslands themselves are at little risk of disappearing—if anything, they are spreading.

Confined mostly to the developing world, where the human population is growing most rapidly, the world's tropical grasslands are under threat. Agriculture, industry, pollution, and urbanization are all playing a part in their transformation. Some areas have turned into farmland, others have become desert, and many are losing their native wildlife.

## Saving the Planet

In Africa, the best hope for conserving savanna wildlife perhaps lies in ecotourism. South Africa, Tanzania, and Kenya attract millions of tourists each year, hoping to catch a glimpse of the "big five": lions, elephants, rhinos, buffalo, and leopards. Kenya's national parks and game reserves are the envy of the world. Tourism was bringing around $400 million each year into Kenya, helping to fund the national parks and giving the government good reason to protect them. However, after the 2007 presidential election, there was a crisis in the country and the number of tourists plummeted. This has led to an increase in poaching in the park. Zambia, Zimbabwe, Madagascar, and Botswana also have ecotourist industries, though those of the latter two countries have, again, suffered in recent years due to political unrest.

*Safari minibuses sometimes outnumber elephants in parts of Kenya's Amboseli National Park. Many park animals are now used to vehicles and ignore them.*

*Though amusing to watch, baboons can be dangerous if they get too close. They often invade cars, campsites, and tourist lodges in search of easy pickings.*

have recently been established to conserve this tree and plant new trees to replace those cut down.

## A Changing Biome

Tropical grasslands are one of the youngest biomes. Since they formed some 20 million years ago, they have fluctuated with changes in Earth's climate, taking territory from forests in dry periods and reverting to forest in wetter times. Like temperate grasslands, tropical grasslands thrive on conflict and change—they flourish in areas that are periodically disturbed, either by fire, people, animals, or extremes of climate.

In some parts of the world, large areas of savanna have existed for thousands of years purely because of human interference. The western part of Madagascar and nearly all of India, for instance, would probably be covered in seasonal tropical forest if they

Tourists do little damage to the savanna **ecosystem**, but they do have an impact. In Kenya's Masai Mara, there are so many jeeps and minibuses following cheetahs that these big cats now find it difficult to hunt in daylight. Baboons and vervet monkeys have become so accustomed to food handouts that they leap on cars and intimidate campers. In the shops and markets, tourists haggle eagerly over the traditional ebony carvings made by the Makonde people, unaware that the trade is killing off the African blackwood tree. Two organizations

*When tropical forests are cut down, grasslands grow in their place. Cattle ranchers have turned large parts of the Amazon rain forest into pasture this way.*

 ## Unequal Benefits

Tourism conserves wildlife most effectively when the profits it generates ends up in the hands of the local people. If locals can see the economic benefits of wild animals, they are more willing to help protect them. In Kenya, however, things have not always worked out this way. Most of the national parks and tourist lodges are run by people belonging to Kenya's Kikuyu community. In the past, the Kikuyu pocketed the profits of tourism, while the Maasai people—in whose homeland the parks are established—got next to nothing. Worse still, the Maasai's grazing rights were restricted, and in some cases people were forcibly relocated. In the 21st century, things are improving and the Maasai now earn a share of the profits.

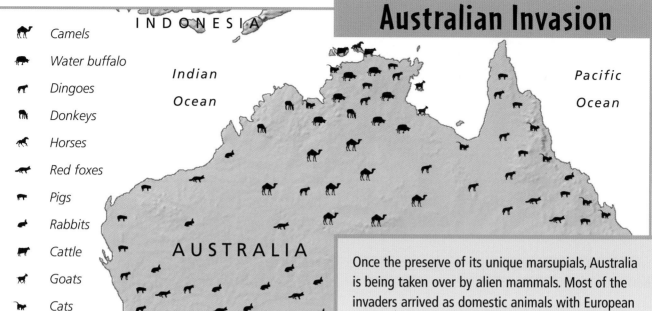

## Australian Invasion

Camels
Water buffalo
Dingoes
Donkeys
Horses
Red foxes
Pigs
Rabbits
Cattle
Goats
Cats

INDONESIA

Indian
Ocean

Pacific
Ocean

AUSTRALIA

Once the preserve of its unique marsupials, Australia is being taken over by alien mammals. Most of the invaders arrived as domestic animals with European colonists but escaped into the wild and survived. First on the scene was the dingo, some 50,000 years ago; it probably drove thylacines to extinction. More recent arrivals include donkeys, buffalo, and camels, brought to Australia as beasts of burden; rabbits and foxes, which were introduced to be hunted; and horses, which were bred by the army. All sorts of farm animals (with the exception of sheep) have escaped into the wild, as have rats, mice, and pet cats. Many of Australia's native mammals seem unable to compete with the invaders and are likely to suffer the same fate as the thylacine.

were uninhabited. The same is true of parts of Southeast Asia, Africa, and northern Australia. In all these places, fire, agriculture, livestock, and collection of wood for fuel all help preserve a kind of artificial savanna.

Such landscapes are spreading. As tropical forests are cut down by farmers, loggers, and cattle ranchers, grasslands are taking their place. In some places, the change may be irreversible. With no trees to soak up and release moisture, the climate can get drier. Humidity drops, fewer clouds form, and there is no longer enough rain for forest. When it does rain, the water simply runs off the dusty ground in sheets, washing away precious soil.

## Introduced Species

The world's wildest tropical grasslands are becoming more uniform. Species introduced from one continent to another sometimes multiply with unexpected speed, taking over from natives. In South America's llanos, for instance, an African grass called jaragua has spread aggressively, replacing native species in huge areas. Besides disrupting the local plant life, alien grasses deprive animals of food if they are less digestible than native

grasses. In Australia, introduced mammals seem better able to survive in the wild than the native marsupials, many of which are now threatened as a result.

## Global Warming

If scientists are right, gases released by human activity are making Earth's climate warmer. Such gases add to the greenhouse effect—like the panes of glass in a greenhouse, they let sunlight in but trap heat rays emitted by the Sun-warmed ground.

The greenhouse effect is a natural process that has been happening for billions of years. In recent times, however, its effects seem to

## Climate Change

There are conflicting theories as to how grasslands might respond to global warming. The raised levels of carbon dioxide in the air might stimulate grassland plants and help them to use water more efficiently, counteracting the effects of drought. Alternatively, desertification might turn grassland to dust, releasing trapped carbon in the soil and making the greenhouse effect worse. The increasing use of fire in grasslands releases even more carbon dioxide. According to some estimates, fires started by people now burn as much as 75 percent of African savanna annually.

*Feral camels in Australia are the descendants of the camels brought over—mainly from India—in the 19th and early 20th centuries for use as beasts of burden. There are now more than 1 million camels in Australia.*

have increased, resulting in what scientists call global warming—an increase in our planet's average temperature. The main cause of global warming is thought to be the gas carbon dioxide, which escapes into the atmosphere when people burn fossil fuels such as wood, coal, and gasoline.

Global warming could force us to redraw the map of biomes. Some parts of the tropics might become drier, causing grasslands to encroach on forest. At the same time, deserts might spread at the expense of grasslands. However, a rise in Earth's temperature would

increase the atmosphere's humidity and bring more rain to some places. Forests might then spread at the expense of grasslands, and grasslands at the expense of deserts.

Whatever the future holds, it seems likely that the grassland biome, in some shape or form, is with us to stay. Perhaps tropical grasslands will move as the climate changes, but they will still exist.

*Ever resourceful, baboons and hyenas sometimes profit from the expanding human population. These two are searching for leftovers in a garbage heap.*

# GLOSSARY

**acacia:** A type of flowering tropical tree common in savannas.

**annual:** A plant that lives for only a year or less (*see also* perennial).

**arid:** Having a very dry climate.

**atmosphere:** The layer of air around Earth.

**biome:** A major division of the living world, distinguished by its climate and wildlife.

**browser:** A herbivore that feeds on trees and shrubs rather than grass (*see also* grazer).

**bulb:** A kind of fattened root used by a plant for storing food.

**camouflage:** Natural disguise that makes animals or plants look like their surroundings.

**canopy:** The rooflike layer of treetops in a forest.

**carbon dioxide:** One of the gases in air. Animals and plants produce carbon dioxide constantly. The gas is also released when fuel burns. It is one of the main gases causing global warming.

**carnivore:** A flesh-eating animal. Carnivore can also mean any member of the Carnivora, an order of mostly flesh-eating mammals.

**climate:** The pattern of weather that happens in one place during an average year.

**cloud forest:** A lush, misty forest found on mountains in the tropics.

**deforestation:** The clearing of forest, usually carried out by cutting down or burning trees.

**desert:** A place where less than 250 millimeters (10 inches) of rain falls a year.

**desertification:** The process of becoming like a desert. It can happen naturally or because of human interference.

**didgeridoo:** A large bamboo or wooden trumpetlike instrument of the Australian Aborigines.

**dormant:** So inactive as to appear lifeless. Plant seeds often stay dormant until their soil gets wet.

**ecosystem:** A collection of living animals and plants that function together with their environment.

**equator:** An imaginary line around Earth, midway between the North and South poles.

**eucalyptus:** A type of plant native to Australia. Eucalyptus trees are also called gum trees.

**evaporate:** To turn into gas. When water evaporates, it becomes water vapor, an invisible part of the air.

**evolve:** To change gradually over many generations. All the world's species have formed through evolution.

**gallery forest:** A strip of forest along a riverbank.

**global warming:** The gradual warming of Earth's climate, caused by pollution of the atmosphere.

**grazer:** A herbivore that mainly eats grass (*see also* browser).

**hemisphere:** One half of Earth. The northern hemisphere is the half that is north of the equator.

**herbivore:** A plant-eating animal.

**hominid:** A member of the family of two-legged apes made up of humans and our fossil ancestors.

**hunter-gatherer:** A person who obtains food by hunting, fishing, and foraging rather than farming.

**ivory:** A hard white material that forms the tusks of elephants.

**mammal:** A warm-blooded animal that feeds its young on milk.

**marsupial:** A type of mammal in which the young develop inside a pouch on the mother's body.

**microclimate:** The pattern of weather within a small area, such as a valley, treetop, or burrow.

**migration:** A journey made by an animal to find a new home. Many animals migrate each year.

**monsoon:** A very rainy season in South Asia; or the wind that causes the rainy season.

**nomad:** A person who travels from place to place in search of food and water, instead of settling permanently.

**nutrient:** Any chemical that nourishes plants or animals, helping them grow. Plants absorb nutrients from the soil, while animals get nutrients from food.

**paleontologist:** A scientist who studies fossils.

**perennial:** A plant that lives for several years (*see also* annual).

**pollen:** Dustlike particles produced by the male parts of a flower.

**predator:** An animal that catches and eats other animals.

**primate:** A type of mammal that usually has grasping hands and forward-facing eyes. Most primates live in the trees of tropical forests.

**protein:** One of the major food groups. It is used for building and repairing plant and animal bodies.

**rain forest:** A lush forest that receives frequent heavy rainfall.

**reptile:** A cold-blooded animal such as a snake, lizard, crocodile, or turtle that usually has scaly skin and moves either on its belly or on short legs.

**ruminant:** An animal with a complex, multichambered stomach. One chamber, the rumen, contains microorganisms that help digest tough plants.

**savanna:** Tropical grassland with scattered trees.

**scrub or scrubland:** Alternative general names for shrubland.

**shrubland:** A biome that mainly contains shrubs, such as the chaparral of California.

**species:** A particular type of organism. Cheetahs are a species but birds are not, because there are lots of different bird species.

**temperate:** Having a moderate climate. Earth's temperate zone lies between the tropics and the polar regions.

**tropic of Cancer:** An imaginary line around Earth 2,600 kilometers (1,600 miles) north of the equator.

**tropic of Capricorn:** An imaginary line around Earth 2,600 kilometers (1,600 miles) south of the equator.

**tropical:** Between the tropics of Cancer and Capricorn. Tropical places are warm all year.

**tropical forest:** Forest in Earth's tropical zone, such as tropical rain forest or monsoon forest.

**tropical grassland:** A tropical biome in which grass is the main form of plant life.

**tundra:** A biome of the far north, made up of treeless plains.

**ungulate:** A type of mammal, such as a horse, elephant, or antelope, that has hooves and eats plants.

# Further Research

## Books
Bright, Michael. *South America Revealed*. New York: DK Publishing, 2001.
Lemasolai-Lekuton, Joseph. *Facing the Lion: Growing Up Maasai on the African Savanna*. Washington, D.C.: National Geographic Children's Books, 2003.
MacDonald, David. *The New Encyclopedia of Mammals*. New York: Oxford University Press, 2001.
Toupin, Laurie. *Savannas: Life In The Tropical Grasslands*. New York: Franklin Watts, 2005.

## Websites
Wild World: www.nationalgeographic.com/wildworld/terrestrial.html
(A National Geographic clickable world map, providing masses of information about the world's ecosystems.)
Tropical Grasslands (Savannah): www.pupilvision.com/uppersixth/savanna1.htm
(Comprehensive information about one of the most famous tropical grasslands.)
Animal Planet: Mammal Guide: animal.discovery.com/guides/mammals/habitat/tropgrassland/overview.html
(Information about the many mammals that live in tropical grasslands.)
Grassland Animals: www.enchantedlearning.com/biomes/grassland/grassland.shtml
(Fun site that includes pictures and information about grassland wildlife.)

# INDEX

Page numbers in *italics* refer to picture captions.

## Picture Credits

Key: l – left, r – right, m – middle, t – top, b – bottom.

**Front Cover:** istockphoto
**Ardea:** 32; D. Parer and E. Parer-Cook 26/27; Hans D. Dossenbach 47b/l; Jean-Paul Ferrero 45t, 46t/r, 56, 57; Ferrero-Labat 1, 28, 44t, 48t; Bob Gibbons 25t; Francois Gohier 8b; Chris Harvey 16; Gunter Kohler 7l; P. Morris 30t; Marc Nanzer 55b; Adrian Warren 6m, 12; M. Watson 53; Bilat Yves 42t/l; **Bruce Coleman:** Sarah Cook 37; Gerald S. Cubitt 24t; Christer Fredriksson 24/25; HPH Photography 35t; Gunter Kohler 7m, 43t; Luiz Claudio Marigo 6r, 20t, 30/31; **Corbis:** Joe McDonald 36t; Penny Tweedie 7r, 19b, 51; **istockphoto:** 61t; **NHPA:** Daryl Balfour 47l, 61b; Anthony Bannister 31t, 38/39 42t/r, 47r; Nigel Dennis 36b; Nick Garbutt 27b; Martin Harvey 18r, 20b, 23; Stephen Krasemann 14t; Harold Palo Jr. 54b; Christophe Ratier 40; Andy Rouse 34/35, 46t/m; Kevin Schafer 46t/l; Jonathan and Angela Scott 18l, 42b; John Shaw 10/11; Dave Watts 45b; **PhotoDisc:** Robert Glusic 4m; Bruce Heinemann 5l; Jack Hollingsworth 5m; Photolink 5r, 19t, Karl Weatherly 4r; Jeremy Woodhouse 41b; **Science Photo Library:** John Durham 22; John Reader 50; **Shutterstock:** Stephane Angue 48b, Tomas Mikolanda 44b, Artur Tiutenko 52b; **Still Pictures:** Dianne Blell 58; M. and C. Denis-Hunt 55t; Mark Edwards 54t, 59b; Nicolas Granier 59t; Fritz Polking 26b; Roland Seitre 8t, 29; Dave Watts 41t. **Thinkstock:** 33b; Stockbyte 14b.

The Brown Reference Group Ltd. has made every attempt to contact the copyright holder. If anyone has any information please contact info@brownreference.com